NICE PEOPLE FINISH FIRST

By Paul H. Wright

For Peter, Gretchen, and Nick

DEDICATION

I am dedicating *Nice People Finish First* to my son, Peter Wright, my daughter Gretchen Horner-Wright, and my younger son, Nicholas Horner-Wright in honor of all that they have given to me and continue to give to me. Peter, being my first- born son, taught me in a very powerful way, by making me a father, how my life had meaning far beyond what I could have understood before. Being his father changed my view of my connection with the universe. He taught me many lessons, particularly the importance of being a rugged individualist while giving to others. Gretchen has shown me how a young woman can be pretty, act so feminine, kind, and loving and still be tough, resourceful, and intellectually astute. Nicholas's energy, courage, sense of humor, love, and loyalty is an inspiration every day as I live and interact with the world around me. Nicholas's dynamic spirit still influences me. Nicholas would have been an intuitive healer in his own right had he lived past 23.

My Thank You To My Mentors and Supporters

I have been fortunate enough to have a number of humble mentors: Dr. Emery Varhely, my clinical supervisor in New York

State, Dr. Richard McClure, my first psychotherapist for six years in New York; Dr. Leon Somers in Andover, Massachusetts, my later therapist who was a mentor to me for 20 years. In recent years, Pastor Alice Ling was a powerful spiritual advisor in my life, as was and is Barry, my sponsor in AA. My parents were often humble mentors. Without these mentors, who were dynamic in their humility, I would not have been able to possess the happiness that I now have, and this book never would have been written.

There were also a number of people who helped edit and supplied helpful suggestions for this book: Richard Gottlieb who I especially enjoyed working with as my professional editor, Leslie Horner-Wright, Fred Bates, Jeffery De Rego, and Gloria Bingel who critiqued my writing. They all worked very hard to help me be more concise and better organized.

A special note of thanks goes to Mark Wright, my brother, who down through the years as this book was slowly developing had very creative input when *Nice People...*" was first conceived twenty years ago. At that time the title was "The Bull's Eye is a Circle" and had to become a little less abstract to be generally useful. He was most helpful in that transition.

purpose

This year marks the 50th year of my work in the mental health field. I'm still working at the age of 77 as a part-time licensed psychologist in Manchester, New Hampshire. I love it! Every one of my clients is unique with many complications because of their special histories and genetic make-up. There are also many different approaches to working on similar clinical issues. However, I'm writing this book because I wanted to share some of the central, universal principles that I've come to recognize as critical to sound mental health and a happy life.

I have had the privilege and pleasure of working with many good people who struggled emotionally for a long time but didn't feel comfortable seeing a psychologist. Coming to my office was often a scary thing for them. Mental health professionals are just human beings going through the same issues that all people go through. Some of what I've written is autobiographical; some of what I've learned has come from my professional training, but most of it has come from the clients I've worked with and the people in my life who were my teachers. This is a summation of what has worked in my life. I hope that these ideas will prove helpful to the reader as well.

Winning is all that is important to many people, but "winning" in the traditional sense doesn't appear to bring enduring serenity and happiness. The phrase, "Nice guys finish last," comes from the sports world. Attributed to the manager of the Brooklyn Dodgers, Leo Durocher, in 1946, it has become extremely popular in the decades since. However, with this as our battle cry, what do we win? How long does the happiness from being number one last? How great would it be to "win" happiness that is enduring and spreads rapidly to everyone we meet? This book is my effort to describe what I consider to be the guiding principles that can be used to rapidly reach the goal of happiness and solid mental health. It introduces a model of mental health which is built on healthy relationships with our selves and others. By working with them daily, people living by these basic principles can create serenity, regardless of the immediate circumstances in their current lives.

I have worked on ideas for this book for many years. However, watching the London Olympics in July 2012 inspired me.

The U.S. women's artistic gymnastics team won the gold medal there, and the team spirit of those young women moved me, reminding me that life itself is a team sport. Those competitive athletes had been supportive of each other. They had been, in a word, nice to each other. I believe that the developing quality of their relationships with each other earned them their place at the top. I could see this in the way that videos of them showed their communication with one another. Constantly encouraging each other, rather than being critical of their teammates' mistakes, they simply made helpful suggestions. That, I believe, genuinely helped them win. In a very tangible way, those young women had won before they won.

Those women will remember their victory in vivid detail for the rest of their lives. However, during their competitions and training they had learned to be good friends by being humble, appreciating each other, loving each other's behaviors, and forgiving each other's mistakes.

These five women, Gabby Douglas, McKayla Maroney, Aly Raisman, Kyla Ross, and Jordyn Wieber, dubbed themselves the

Fierce Five. Their close-knit relationship led them to support each other as they confronted the sexual abuse experienced by female gymnasts that year at the hands of Dr. Lawrence Gerard Nassar. It took a lot of courage for young women to testify in this kind of sexual abuse case. On May 16, 2018, they were awarded the Arthur Ashe Courage Award for their part in exposing the abuse.

I firmly believe that, for all of us, the enemies of solid mental health are negative emotions that develop from feelings that tell us that we must face life alone. The barriers of good mental health are not the difficult people, places, or events that come our way. It is only when we confront these difficulties without loving support that we have real emotional problems.

We defeat stress in our lives every day when we work in a loving cooperative manner with our fellow human beings to meet the challenges of our lives. In other words, we defeat emotional stress by improving the quality of our relationships with ourselves and with others. This book is about the steps we can take to improve those relationships. What I will be discussing here is what I consider to be the universal tools or ways of governing all our actions to keep us happy and productive. I believe that using these tools will enable us to rid ourselves of negative emotions and be more productive, serene and truly happy and, in other words, "finish first." If being productive and *happy* are our chosen goals, I believe that there are five principles that together form the key.

Each moment that we're alive involves a choice for our state of mind, e.g., to be happy or depressed; to be creative, loving and serene; or to be angry and depressed. If we put the quality of our relationships first, I believe, we will be happy. If we don't, then the choice can be made for rather than by us. Negative habits of thinking and behaving will bring us down. When we consciously choose to love ourselves and others without conditions, we can be happy and serene. This book outlines clear principles that work toward this goal of happiness regardless of a person's age, sex, or financial status. The principles discussed below have, I think, endured since human beings first appeared on this earth. The principles of *Humility*; *Appreciation*; *Love*; *Forgiveness*; and, finally, *Spirituality* discussed here are the building blocks of a happy and meaningful life. I define these five principles in the following manner:

- *Humility* – A sense that my value as a person is equal to everyone else's, whether they be rich or poor, educated or uneducated, powerful or not, and so forth.

- *Appreciation* – The focus on what is valuable in me and in all people and events around me in spite of inevitable imperfections.

- *Love* – Acting in a manner that produces physical and/or mental health in self and others.

- *Forgiveness* – Dealing with others and ourselves especially as we are now, regardless of how we were in the past and letting go of resentments toward ourselves and others for injurious past behavior.

- *Spirituality* – Believing that we are a part of an eternal reality that is not matter but pure, loving and creative energy. Believing that we are not merely matter but that we truly do matter.

I refer to these throughout this book as the H.A.L.F.S. Principles.

When I got my graduate degree in 1970 and later my license as a psychologist, I had a surprising realization. Those two accomplishments meant a great deal to me, and I was ecstatic for a while until a slight depression set in and a voice inside me asked, "Is that all there is?" If you have ever worked hard to reach a specific goal and achieved it, you may have had this experience yourself. My perception changed when I saw these achievements as tools to help others.

Unlike such linear achievements (degrees, promotions, raises, etc.), the happiness that we can derive from our relationships with our family and friends is on-going. It will, of course, include a few wrinkles. There will almost certainly be temporary conflicts.

In our world, being a goal-directed person is the standard. This is deeply embedded in our culture. It can be a good thing, but, when relationships take a back seat to competitive attitudes over issues such as money, prestige or power, we have a big problem.

This book is about how to receive with gratitude and give generously, and with this cycle cultivate happiness. Happiness begins when we use our head. We must constantly choose to be grateful and generous to be truly happy and love ourselves and others equally. If we can do this, experience has taught me, we tend to achieve more of our tangible linear goals such as better financial security and greater education. However, we must choose our priorities carefully.

Psychologists did not invent the principles of mental health. The four principles and the concept of a spiritual life are a gift from God. They're the inheritance of us all and have been with people since the beginning of human life. The purpose of *Nice People Finish First* is to highlight the five ancient concepts mentioned above which allow us to choose to focus on acting with gratitude and generosity. I'll discuss the history and application of these concepts later in this book in the chapters named after each principle. When we behave in concert with them, we will experience a serene and happy life.

Introduction

Ever since I was a Senior Narcotics Rehabilitation Counselor in 1970, I have been asking myself: "Are there be some basic simple rules that keep people emotionally healthy and happy?" Not everybody wants to study psychology or even needs go to church to have principles to live by. There have always been people who have never experienced psychotherapy who have them nonetheless, of course. I regularly see new clients who are atheists who have been asked by someone who loves them to come to counseling. Some of these people have never even thought about doing so but have a particular problem that someone significant feels that counseling could help resolve.

One highly intelligent man whose wife was expecting their third child was facing a crisis over whether he would be a good father. This nervous father was worried about whether the effects of the poor parenting that he had received in his childhood had led him and would with his unborn child lead him further to make bad choices as a father. In every other major area of his life he was emotionally healthy. He always helped others in every way that he could and volunteered regularly to cook at the local food pantry. I reminded him a number of times how his current altruistic life-style would have a powerful example for his children. In addition, that because of his humility, he was willing to learn better ways of disciplining his children. He also became aware that his ability to enjoy his children was something his father never expressed to him while he was growing up. I suggested that if he continued to learn because of his humility, truly appreciate himself and his children, do loving things for himself and his children, and forgive his children and himself for mistakes that they made, his children would be healthy and happy. As the weeks went by, he could see how his first two children had begun to thrive, and his confidence grew. Unlike many parents who do repeat the treatment they experienced as children, he was able to stop history from repeating itself. He was so anxious about making mistakes before therapy, that he hadn't noticed how his first two were thriving before he had started therapy and that he had reason to believe that his third child would probably thrive as well.

What I have noticed in the 50 years that I have been in the mental health profession is that people who are kind to themselves tend to be nice to others. We need to love ourselves with a passion equal to that we feel for those around us whom we love. If I am healthy by being nice to myself, then I will have healthy, loving, relationships in my life. Being kind to myself in this context myself means thoroughly enjoying moderate recreational spending, eating delicious but nutritious food and drink, and enjoying other pleasures that do no harm. It also means relating to others in such a manner that we can see the beauty in the changes our relationships produces. Going overboard, being gluttonous or selfish, almost always leads to poor relationships eventually. Ironically, indiscriminate self-sacrifice usually leads to self-loathing. If we are constantly sacrificing for a goal or killing ourselves in order to be a "people pleaser," then we neglect our need for exercise, proper rest, recreation, nutrition, and other essentials for life. By constantly denying ourselves for others, we can reach the point where we have nothing else to sacrifice, and the self-loathing begins.

For me, the first example of being nice to myself was to give up drinking when I realized that I had become an alcoholic. This action brought me increased mental acuity and physical health and energy. It also put me at peace with the conflict that was inside me between what I found very pleasant and what I knew was unhealthy. Others benefitted from my sobriety. I became happier, healthier, and more able to help others become happier and healthier.

The second example of being nice (kind) to myself was to work as a psychotherapist pro- bono on a weekly basis, with an emotionally distraught person who had become unemployed and had no means of paying for treatment. It was a rewarding experience for my client, I believe, and certainly for me. We both became happier. I enjoyed helping my client, and he enjoyed being free from his depression. For me, being sober meant that I also had more to give others as a husband, father, friend, and psychotherapist. Donating my training as a therapist also made me feel productive by contributing to the improved quality of someone else's life. Being kind in these ways are win-win situations. Everyone benefits from the kindness because everyone involved in the situation is energized by the resultant relationships, and we begin to lose the restlessness that accompanies loneliness.

The real trick to finishing the goal of better relationships is to be humble and to see ourselves as equal in importance as are those to whom we are being kind. We need to be as kind to ourselves as we are to others. Sometimes saying "no" to unreasonable demands from people we care about is the only way to be nice to both ourselves *and* others. However, refusing unreasonable demands must never mean withdrawing love from others; it means, rather, rejecting certain ideas and behaviors which hurt us and others.

To be nice to ourselves sometimes means being willing to endure pain while we act on our sense of what is healthy. I have been in this position many times with other people who frequently want to borrow money and not pay it back. Saying no to our kids when they are dying to have something that we know is bad for them is being kind in a healthy manner even if they are angry with us temporarily.

Between a Rock and a Hard Place

One evening in December, as I was watching the Jay Leno show, his guest, Aaron Ralston, spoke about his near-death experience while hiking in Utah in 2003. I had an epiphany. This man was discussing his reason for living: loving relationships. Ralston's memoir, *Between a Rock and a Hard Place*, tells the story of a hiking trip that he took in a remote area of the country, far from cell phones and people. As Ralston was climbing a mountain, a boulder fell down and jammed his right arm against a crevasse in the rocks.

Stranded for days in total isolation without food or water, Ralston concluded that the only way to get free was to sacrifice his trapped arm. His only tool was a pocket knife which he'd dulled by trying to scrape away the rock that was trapping him. When the dull blade failed to cut through his arm bone, he used leverage to break the bone using the boulder as a fulcrum.

Ralston said that what kept him going was the image of his family. Wanting to be with them again and an image of a child who might be born into it in the future spurred him on. His vision of being with his family and his unborn son were very vivid and stoked a powerful drive to renew the loving relationships with his family members. This dual vision drove him through the agony of his pinned and shredded arm, hunger, thirst, and fear of death. Ralston's overwhelming drive to renew his loving relationships was stronger than the pain of literally sacrificing his arm. With a dull knife he cut the flesh of his arm and broke its bones. He told of the smile that came to his face when his hand broke away and he was free to go home.

He had learned that what was most important to him were his loving relationships. This was the force that made his life meaningful, not his highly functioning, athletic body. In Ralston's case, being kind to himself meant enduring physical pain to gain the possibility of a full life. Just as a footnote, Ralston and his wife did have a son later as he had hoped; something that never would have happened if he had not endured the pain of survival so that he could be with his family.

Nice People Finish First is founded on the four principles mentioned above: *Humility*, *Appreciation*, *Love*, and *Forgiveness*. Often, and we might hope, a fifth ethic, *Spirituality*, develops which helps drive this approach to mental health. The time I have spent living by these five principles has made it possible for me at age 77 to greet the clear majority of my days with a smile, embrace both my mistakes and successes, and just enjoy being alive. Even more important, I have seen these principles work for so many of my clients when they have used them to guide their actions.

I've struggled with the deaths of several close relatives and friends including my father, step-father, mother, and a son. I have been divorced, experienced foreclosure on a house, faced down bankruptcy, fought with the IRS, recovered from active alcoholism, and once arrived to find an eviction notice on my office door. I've learned and grown from these events and, I hope, have become a better psychotherapist and a friend not only to others but also to myself. My attempts at living according to the H.A.L.F. principles led to a developing spiritual point of view (the fifth principle). This fifth principle has helped me overcome some of these obstacles in my life in a more complete manner.

Giving and Receiving

One of the generalities that I've learned during my years in the mental health field is that healthy people have a balance between giving and receiving in their lives. Healthy giving that encourages health and happiness in others gives *us* an immediate return in terms of joy and tranquility. An example of this might be volunteering your time to read to a bedridden child. Unhealthy giving sacrifices

16

things that we shouldn't sacrifice such as working an extra 10 or 20 hours a week so that our children can have everything—no matter how insignificant—that their hearts desire. This type of giving brings anxiety, depression, and poor health.

Being receptive to the good things around us (such as emotional support from others in a time of crisis) is of equal importance. If we are truly humble, we realize that, being equal in worth, we are like those we try to help, allowing us to more easily receive the help that we need when we need it. Unfortunately, in my experience people in the so-called helping professions often develop an unrealistic frame of mind that says that we don't need the help that other people do. To be healthy, we need to be humble, seeing ourselves as having the same needs as everyone else and therefore able to receive the help that we need with gratitude. This humble receptivity enables us to have much more to give.

Our early family life with accepting, responsible parents can be a fantastic, lasting foundation for a healthy life. We can more easily learn to be humble and therefore balance healthy giving and receiving. My parents had their own flaws (as do all parents). Some of the lessons that I learned in my childhood such as the necessity of always having to be perfect, I had to discard. However, my parents loved me and gave me a sense of what was right and wrong, and from that a basic foundation of values. Not everyone is so fortunate. The less fortunate need to find parental figures who have meaningful lives to emulate. That could be a teacher or a coach, for example. Ironically, grandparents, who raised their own children who ultimately lacked those good parental attributes, are often these wise parental figures.

While it is true there were times that I left some of my parents' good teachings in the dust to do my own thing – being obsessed with achievement and falling into alcoholism; in later years I could return to the values that gave me strength and stability. The H.A.L.F. principles and Spirituality were taught to me in many ways by my parents' example as they raised me. This book revisits those values that are the core of my happiness.

Although our families of origin can teach us much about relationships, it is wise to develop a circle of friends who help fill the gap between what we need and what our families can offer. It is the quality of the relationships in our primary and secondary families that is such a help to us in our journey to become fully self-actualized. I measure the quality of these relationships by the extent to which they demonstrate: humility, appreciation, love and forgiveness.

I loved working with people at Derry Counseling Service, an experience which lasted 38 years. I have learned so much about people and the world around me from my colleagues, and gained inspiration from clients who have survived situations I've never had to face.

I had begun my private practice in Derry in 1975 under the supervision of Dr. Jesus Morea, a psychologist, until 1988, when I became a New Hampshire Certified Associate Psychologist. (I became a Licensed Psychologist in1993.) As a certified associate psychologist, I could practice independently.

During these professional experiences, I observed my clients' lives, coming to recognize that they were healthy and happy when they lived by the H.A.L.F. principles and that they became anxious, depressed, angry and functioning poorly when they didn't,.

Spirituality

I talked to my eldest son, Peter, recently (from 2000 miles away in a field outside Lawrence, Kansas) about my most recent work on this book. He commented that I had come full circle with my thinking, moving from spiritual to psychological and back to spiritual. In tracing the path of my journey through the writing process, I realized that he was right.

Some people's experience in life may make it temporarily impossible for them to become spiritual. They become too skeptical to have spiritual views. If that is the case, it is my experience that following the H.A.L.F. principles often leads to a spiritual view later in life. If someone does not become more spiritually minded, these principles in their actions will lead to a happier life nevertheless. Despite my many years as a mental health professional, it has been mainly my developing spiritual life that has pulled me through grim times. Knowledge of my own psychological issues helped, but it didn't dissipate my fears of death, of being alone, or of economic and professional failure. When I focused on my supportive family, friends, loving relationships, and my faith in God, my fears began to disappear. It is our loving relationships that keep us strong.

What if we could reduce all our fears to a minimum? How can we minimize fear and be at peace? We can't do this alone. However, we can minimize these fears if we have loving connections with others, our inner self, and a higher power. We also need to be certain that these loving connections are our primary reason for being alive. To remain emotionally healthy, we cannot allow ourselves to put our ambitions or temporary signs of security (material wealth) ahead of our loving relationships. If we keep our priorities in line, death itself becomes less fearsome.

We live in such a task-oriented culture that having good relationships as a primary goal for a lifetime is often seen as insufficient. Unfortunately, accumulated wealth, property, or influence often appear more important, and the fear of losing these things often leads to anxiety and depression. Living by the H.A.L.F. principles can help us create and maintain our goal of healthy relationships. Living this way often develops spirituality, which in turn, strengthens our use of the H.A.L.F. principles. Wealth, education, popularity, and station in life do not give us enduring happiness; feeling a loving connection does. The loving connection can be through any of the senses; the touch of a reassuring hand, the sound of comforting words, or the sight of an empathetic expression. It can also be experienced through vivid memories of loved ones.

Psychotherapy

Many people fear psychotherapy. That fear need not prevent them from dealing with emotional problems. I have noticed a clear pattern of what successfully helps people with their emotional issues even when they cannot attend psychotherapy. My approach to mental health focuses on helping people improve the quality of their connections with their inner selves as well as with others. This connection is the key to our happiness and success in life. *Nice people reach this goal of happiness first.*

All of us have a need for a framework or a philosophy of mental health to give direction to our day-to-day reality. The internet dictionary gives one definition of a philosophical attitude as one of composure and calm in the presence of trial and annoyances. *Nice People Finish First* is an attempt at articulating a philosophy of life that leads to composure in the presence of trials and annoyances.

Admittedly, I myself do not always live by this philosophy because I am noticeably imperfect and at times do allow my irritations and fears to creep in. However, when I follow these rules, my life is serene and happy.

Specific mental health issues such as agoraphobia or social phobia are often the results of the philosophy of life which we develop during childhood. Ideas such as unforgiveable sins, or that liking yourself is being selfish, or the belief that nothing short of perfection is acceptable are concepts often deeply imbedded in children's consciousness. They can prove to be very destructive, and people often need some kind of intervention (it doesn't necessarily need to be therapy) to uproot them. Broad ideas like the importance of learning new things from our mistakes and relying on a trusted support system when times get tough are extremely important.

Whether we are Christians, Buddhists, Muslims, or atheists, the four principles mentioned above appear to be universal and eternal. Buddhists believe that it is only with a humble mind that we can see and overcome our short comings. St Augustine wrote, "Almost the whole of Christian teaching is humility." The Quran teaches that every aspect of Mohamed's life reflected humility whether he was walking. talking, sitting, or eating.

Christianity talks at length about appreciation in the form of gratitude. The Buddhist teacher Jack Kornfield writes about the psychological value of being grateful for life's challenges that give us the means of self-improvement. Gratitude is considered a form of worship for Muslims.

About love, in the New Testament the Apostle Paul states that, regardless of our gifts, without love, our gifts and efforts are useless. Buddha's writings, stress that love, compassion, joy, and equanimity are the very nature of an enlightened person. They describe the necessity of an unconditional love. Muslims believe that God created love as a necessary instinct that we need to manifest in the world around us.

As for forgiveness, Christianity describes the relationship of forgiving others and its relationship to feeling forgiven mentioned clearly in The Lord's Prayer: "Forgive us our transgressions as we forgive those who transgress against us." The Buddhist scholar Sri Sri Ravi Shankar writes that "the person whom you are forgiving should not even be aware that you are forgiving them." In other words, saying, "I forgive you," makes other people aware of their error, which is to be ignored. The Quran talks about God's unconditional forgiveness and calls on its followers to be forgiving to those who hurt them.

Conducting our lives guided by humility, appreciation, love, and forgiveness often leads to a life that is spiritual and brings us peace. It is my belief that, if our actions are guided by these principles, what develops is a rich life. We become deeply connected to our best selves and to those around us.

If we have lost a someone we loved but can keep in good contact with the other loved ones around us, we can find peace and a resolution of our grief. Mourning takes time to resolve, and we need to be humble enough to realize that there are others who have been through similar tragedies and been healed. We also must appreciate and accept the love and support of others who have weathered similar storms of pain. Outside of our personal circle of family and friends, grief support groups can be a tool that a grieving people can use to help others who are mourning while they receive help for their grief. We need to continue to actively do loving things for ourselves and others. While this is not easy to do if we are depressed, it's important to forgive ourselves and the person we have lost for what we both did and didn't do that harmed the relationship.

This is a big order, but I've seen it work again and again. As part of my training, I spent a couple of years as a member of a generic therapy group. During that time, I saw a number of group members overcoming a wide variety of losses: the loss of someone they loved, losses of careers, and sometimes losses of physical health just by sharing their emotional pain. In my case, the pain I needed to heal was the death of my father with whom I had a conflictual relationship. I believe a healthy life isn't so complicated to understand, but at times, however, it takes great discipline to live by the H.A.L.F. principles. Living by these principles requires challenging work, but the prize is well worth it.

Fear and Paranoia Creates Bad Health

I must credit many of the personality theorists that I have been exposed to for my developing ideas on mental health. One of these is Karen Horney, who felt that the fear of being cut off from love was the universal fear that creates ill health. A good example of that was a client of mine who walked through my door 20 years ago.

A clergyman, he had lived through his mother's suicide when he was

a child, which left him feeling of being unloved and unlovable.

However, he was angry with and lashed out at any woman who tried

to be close to him or with whom he tried to form a relationship. This

anger was constant with the very people who could have helped him

overcome his fear of not ever being loved, which, not surprisingly,

left him unhappy. From what I could tell, he gave good sermons and

was an able church administrator, but he got close to no one. His

anxiety over this seemingly unresolvable problem—he couldn't go

back and resolve the issue with his mother or unlive the shock of

losing her in that way—led to obsessive compulsiveness. He

couldn't leave his house without checking the locks on his doors at

least five times.

To me the fear of being cut off from love very often comes

from extremely harsh self-criticism. Sometimes children develop this

harsh self-criticism on their own if they do not get enough consistent

structure from parents who nurture them. Sometimes this develops

from a critical parent. The feeling, however, is the same. "If I am not good enough, I won't be loved and/or respected." From harsh self-criticism comes isolation. We feel that we cannot face our own faults because they are too numerous. Denial (this happens subconsciously) of a person's own shortcomings seems to occur next out of fear of being seen as unworthy of love and respect. To help with this denial, projection (subconsciously seeing the other person with our faults) can occur, and, as a defense, we begin to feel superior to others. This happens when we begin looking at the flaws in others so that we can deny our own flaws. From this dynamic comes emotional cut-offs from people who don't like being criticized. Out of this, more isolation and a state of general paranoia can develop. When people say, "I trust nobody," this usually includes themselves), that person's paranoid attitude puts great pressure on a person and creates a tremendous amount of anxiety and depression The self-criticality (mentally beating on ourselves) becomes paranoia. The fear of isolation tends to bring about isolation, a self-fulfilling prophecy. The hypothetical person may begin thinking: "I'll reject you because I know you'll reject me".

We need to feel forgiven and accepted for who and what we

are right now. We can choose to do this. In my view, a belief in unconditional love is at the core of true spirituality. When we can truly love the person that we are right now, paranoia begins to disappear. When we stop beating ourselves up with criticism, our criticism of others tends to diminish. This is easier using the H.A.L.F.S. principle as a point of reference to guide our view of ourselves and the world around us. Psychotherapy and/or strongly spiritual people can assist us in this difficult change. The psyche needs to be re-conditioned in this manner to develop this outlook as a way of life.

The Why and How to Live

It is my hope that through this text I can suggest principles of how to live more productively. However, before we can do this, we also need to discuss why we are alive. Psychology talks more about the how-to questions, and philosophy talks more about the why's of life. The why-stuff does, in many ways, get its foundation from faith or belief. It is my suggestion that being able to decide our purpose for living is essential to lasting happiness.

I can remember in one of my undergraduate philosophy

seminars at American University discussing proofs for the existence of God. I recall my comment at that time was: "either you believe in God or you don't." It is simply a choice. There will always be alternative beliefs to explain the universe. However, I know that what I believe comes from my being a pragmatist. I believe in a loving, all-forgiving God because doing so works. This belief works by producing an outlook that makes us healthier, highly functioning, and truly happy. Believing in a completely accepting higher power is, I believe, the ultimate connection that can bring a sense of peace, security, and continuity. This choice to believe has clearly helped many an alcoholic get sober, as a study published in *The Alcoholism Treatment Quarterly* (2000, vol. 18) suggests. Research by Betty Jarusiewicz, Ph.D., concluded that "[r]recovering individuals have a statistically greater levels of faith and spirituality than those who tend to relapse."

Being Present in the Present

Being centered in the here-and-now is essential to living according to these principles. It is in the present tense that we can have the power to change things, mostly ourselves. Trying to plan the perfect life or being lost in the failures or successes of the past, we lose focus on the present, and anxiety and depression creep in. This is not to say that we don't need to learn from the past and plan for the future, but the primary effort and energy need to be focused in the present. Life moves very fast. Only by focusing primarily on the present can we truly appreciate our lives and those around us.

Living Spiritually, the Fifth Ethic?

When we lack a faith in what we cannot control, our psychological world can become anxiety-ridden because we are afraid of what may be uncontrollable. An example of this might mean not getting an operation for a cancer treatment because we don't know the outcome. Another more common example is the fear of making a commitment in a relationship because we might get hurt. We can become very afraid of reaching out beyond our own circumscribed psychological world. A small psychological world can produce an unhealthy mind. Good things do often happen when we're not in control, and the mind that refuses to deal with anything not in its control tends to be an anxious and depressed one which can become a mind of complete despondency. There are people without faith who resign themselves to accept things out of their control, but it has been my experience that many of those who resign themselves and lack belief in something larger than themselves find it more difficult to remain calm when things spin out of their control. A belief in a loving and forgiving higher power can reduce this anxiety.

Living according to the ethics of the H.A.L.F. principles is still effective in directing a good life without a belief in God. As an atheist, I can deal with the uncontrollable with an attitude of resignation. However, I do feel that not having a spiritual grounding makes a good life more difficult. I also believe that most of the time, if someone lives according to the four H.A.L.F. principles, they develop a sense of a Higher Power and the value of spirituality. It seems difficult for some people to look at life spiritually. I have noticed that, when people I know decide to believe that what is spiritual is real, their minds become much more peaceful. When we stay in a spiritual relationship with all that is around us, we are less angry, anxious, and depressed and have more energy. It occurs to me that this seems to be a natural healthy state and that only when we deviate from it do we become unhappy.

CHAPTER I: PRIORITIES

We have many decisions to make on a daily basis. The only way that I know to organize my life to make good decisions is to have a system of priorities for my thoughts and actions. We are flooded with problems and can easily suffer from stimulus overload. It is easy to feel very confused: anxious, depressed, and downright overwhelmed. As a priority, I believe in putting the quality of our relationships first. The quality of the relationships we have and/or seek to have is dependent on the balance of giving and receiving which is established in these relationships and which enriches our lives and the lives of others.

We can make many mistakes and lose many tangible possessions and still maintain a stable, happy life if the quality of our relationships remains good. The quality of our relationships is based on living according to the H.A.L.F. principles.

Many of us have important goals in life such as a better education, financial security, or improving a chosen vocation. These goals give us a sense of direction. Let's identify these goals with a lower-case "g." Goals, spiritual Goals, or Goals with a more intangible reward, are more important than our other goals. The upper-case "Goals" are relationship Goals which give our lives meaning and a sense of wellbeing.

Getting a good education, which can be used as a tool to improve our ability to help others, our children, our significant other, and our clients, connects education to the Goal of having a satisfying life. Having a good education for vain reasons such as more power, pride, or status may lead to disaster. Being wealthy for the purpose of helping the less fortunate is a positive thing. In this case, many people may still be hurt if this person's wealth is achieved through radical overachieving competition that might hurt others. Relationships still need to take priority in process of achieving wealth, regardless of how this wealth is spent later.

Loving ourselves and others equally is what I consider the central Goal of a satisfying life. In this state I am not narcissistic, pleasing myself at another's expense. I am not sacrificing my own basic physical and/or emotional needs to please others. The foundation of this satisfying life of loving is humility; considering myself as of *equal* importance to those around me.

Communication

We easily connect with so many people through technology today. However, the quality of the communication needs to be governed by ethical principles that keep our relationships healthy. This needs to be communication that is caring if it is to bring happiness and fulfillment.

There are many different approaches to psychotherapy. However, one factor in using all these different approaches that seems to be universally effective is a warm, safe communication between therapist and client. Most of the time we don't need a psychotherapist to have natural "psychotherapy" through thoughtful communication. Day-to-day, for all of us, it is having a warm, safe relationship between ourselves and many people around us that will create that "therapy" to keep us healthy and growing daily.

Victor Frankl was a psychiatrist who was a Jewish prisoner of war at Auschwitz during World War II. During his suffering, he said that the most significant truth "for all mankind is that love is the ultimate and the highest goal to which man can aspire." Frankl's meaning in life was to help others find theirs. I agree with Frankl that our mental health and happiness is dependent on a life that improves the lives of others. If we follow the five principles that I've already enumerated, we keep our communication with ourselves and others healthy. This process will improve the lives of others. We need to apply them in our communications on a our daily basis to maintain our loving perspective. Just thinking about the five is not enough.

Humility is the foundation of mental health more than any other principle because it is only through humility that we can truly appreciate, love, and forgive ourselves and others. If we're humble, we realize that our value as a person is never greater or less than anyone else's. Love and forgiveness of self and others, in turn, helps us to have a close relationship with our universe – very simply put, we may begin accepting something greater than ourselves.

Spirit is the loving energy that is present in everyone. When we connect with this spirit in others, we begin to grow emotionally healthy. I have worked with felons and people with very serious emotional problems. However, given some time to establish a rapport, I can usually sense the loving spirit in most of these people. What keeps this spiritual light from being *immediately* obvious is a series of pathological defenses we all develop over the years to deal with the fear of being disrespected and alone.

Touching the Lives of Others

There is a woman by the name of Amma whose life is devoted primarily to literally *touching people*. Amma is Hindu but accepts some of the religious practices of all religions as a path to happiness. She says: "Jiamusi (liberation while alive) is not something to be attained after death, nor is it to be experienced or bestowed upon you in another world. It is a state of perfect awareness and equanimity, which can be experienced here and now in this world while living in this body. These souls… merge with the infinite consciousness." Amma has physically embraced 29 million people since 1970. This practice is called *darshan*. When people have been hugged by her, they have often felt healed, their anxiety and pain gone.

While I am not Hindu nor am I in the habit of hugging my clients (even if, at times I think it might help them) I do believe that this sense of emotional connection, like that which the people touched by Amma feel, is what brings true emotional health.

Traditionally, women in our culture converse with people they know just to connect, and, in contrast, often men tend to talk to others to get things done (or about sports). This more female motivation for conversing may, in the long run be healthier. Psychologically, it doesn't seem to matter much what subject is being discussed, if both people feel a loving connection when they talk; unless they're talking to criticize someone else, that connection is the important thing. Quite simply, a loving connection with others is the priority. Isolation brings ill health; it's an excruciating form of punishment for the human soul.

A Sense of Direction and a Sense of Permanency

Do you ever ask the question, "Why am I alive?" If so, does your answer satisfy you? As a psychotherapist, I know that being able to answer that question can be very instrumental in shaping a meaningful and happy life. We have a built-in need for a sense of direction or purpose for our lives. We also seem to have a need for a sense of permanency and continuity. Seeing ourselves as primarily spiritual and connected to what is eternal satisfies the need for permanency.

All the psychotherapeutic techniques that I know of (and I am sure that there are ones that I don't know of) will not, in my humble opinion, keep my clients happy and healthy without some self-knowledge of why their life is important. If our purpose is too narrow (i.e. raise healthy children) then we risk losing that sense of permanency because most of life is change. Our children will become adults. Sometimes changes – financial loss, death of a pivotal loved one, or loss of a career – can shut us off from our sense of purpose and bring a loss of direction, a disconnection to eternity, and unhappiness.

In my view, our purpose is to be creatively connected or to have a harmonious relationship with what is within and around us. We need to have a healthy connection with our bodies, souls, family, friends, and, indeed, the universe that we live in. Most significantly, we need to relate to our spirit – a higher power, what the people in Alcoholics Anonymous call the "God of our own understanding." This would be the God of all religions and one who exists where there is no religion. Religion is a manmade tool for worshipping a higher power. Because it is manmade, it can have many shortcomings. We do not have to be religious to be spiritual.

Living by the four ethical principles – Humility, Appreciation, Love, and Forgiveness – can make this spiritual connection possible. When I speak of a Higher Power, I am aware that I may encourage atheists and agnostics to stop reading. However, it's been my experience that without a spiritual life, mental health is more difficult to maintain.

I realize that I do have to be careful not to offend or in any way be judgmental toward people in my life (some of them highly ethical and functioning) who are atheists. I do believe that people who do not believe in God can be wonderful, happy people. But I also know that there are times when there is no one to talk to and that being able to pray to the universal spirit of love (or God, as I know it) is a great comfort to many of us. I do not believe that this universal spirit controls us or makes all the bad and good things happen in the world. What I do believe is that there is a God who will give us the strength and the wisdom to handle the heavy burdens in our lives and can make us feel whole if we are open to Him (Her?). To me, God is a spirit of love, forgiveness, serenity, and strength.

At one time I saw spirituality as the frosting on a cake; however, in the last three years spirituality has become the cake. Dealing with the untimely death of my son, Nick, forced me to realize that a strong faith can help us to recover from the most painful of tragedies. Wikipedia, (the reader-edited encyclopedia), features an interesting discussion of Victor Frankl who survived four Nazi concentration camps. Death and suffering were an everyday experience for him and his fellow prisoners. The article reads: "Frankl is a man who reminded modern psychology of one detail it had overlooked, the patient's *soul*." During a very low moment during his imprisonment, he became very aware of his psychological, non-material connection with his wife. At that point he began to feel at peace. This experience led to a good deal of his thinking about the healing force that is love, the truly spiritual connection that gave him a reason to live.

For many people, a belief in a loving spiritual entity that unifies all of life works well to encourage mental health. We meet the need for continuity when we have a view of ourselves as primarily spirit and only secondarily physical. We begin to see the purpose of our material being is to house our spirits.

Any ethical or spiritual view must be broad enough to include all mankind and straightforward enough for most people to understand. It is my opinion that any religious or spiritual belief system that views "others" as unworthy of equal treatment is not truly spiritual. The supreme spiritual entity that I believe in treats the most "imperfect" ones as equal in value to any of the others.

One of the basic approaches to scientific thinking is Occam's razor, which states that "all things being equal, the simplest solution tends to be the right one." I believe that all the major religions have some simple common principles that bring out the best mental health in us. Psychology didn't invent mental health. Before psychology, philosophy and religion helped to keep people emotionally sound.

Amma, in her spiritually simple message, hugs people, conveying the message to those that she touches that she loves them and they are loved simply because they are human. There is psychological research that has been done with animals where they are placed in stressful situations. The researchers found that the stress placed on animals in demanding situations was reduced by gentle human touch. The idea of actively producing stress in an animal bothers me ethically. However, some of this research validates Amma's approach. These experimental animals tended to deal with the stress of their environment far better if they are physically stroked in an affectionate manner.

Hugs and affectionate touch have always been a way of communicating care and healing between two living things. Differences in age, cultural backgrounds and even species can make healing of another difficult or impossible. If there is not too much fear between the hugger and the "huggee," i.e., the person being hugged, the hug can communicate unconditional love and be immensely healing both spiritually and physically. Embraces clearly demonstrate the scientific principle that *what is simple can also be profound*. Gentle touch is one way of expressing unconditional love that can be expressed when language, culture and, at times even species may be very different. This gentle touch is one of the ways that we as humans can give and receive unconditional love. I firmly believe that all people can understand that unconditional love. It is a simple example of God's unconditional love that is simply expressed through us humans in that manner.

Freedom and Bondage

We all want to feel free, unencumbered and at peace. However, rules, obligations and routines can bind us. On the other hand, this external structure can reduce our anxiety and depression temporarily. Adhering to rigid structure can also help us feel like "good people" even though we're bound by those rules. The Four Ethical Principles and a strong belief in spirit that these principles encourage offer a structure that is internal rather than external. Living by them enables us to be creative and helps us lead more peaceful lives, less emotionally bound by the ordinary routine "shoulds" of our culture.

Instead of being a law-abiding citizen, I end up being a man who *enjoys* doing things that promote the wellbeing of others. In this case my life goes beyond just being "law abiding." By leading my life humbly, I appreciate the circle of loving and being loved and can forgive myself and others for our mistakes. I am free.

Living according to the four ethical principles very often

leads to a strong belief in a spiritual life that is eternal. This, in turn, leads to less fear of death which becomes merely the cessation of a physical body which houses an eternal soul which is eventually set free. This belief in the eternal soul, to complete the circle, makes it easier to live by the four ethics. The result is a foundation for life that is based on these now *five* principles, which offer a great deal of freedom while giving us direction and structure for a fulfilling, happy life.

With simple rules, freedom tends to be in harmony with the laws of the land. This way of life enables me to feel much more comfortable about two inevitable facts: death and taxes. Death that follows a fulfilling life becomes the opportunity to join more completely with my loved ones who have passed on. Paying taxes becomes a means of helping others to a better life.

Discussing God

Embracing the Four Ethics allows us to conceptualize: spirit, God or a "Higher Power". I am very familiar with Alcoholics Anonymous. It is a fantastic organization that has saved many lives, including my own. Much of the time when a newly sober person begins the AA twelve-step program, he or she discovers that by *choosing* to believe, they can stay sober and that, when they don't believe, it is much more difficult.

Discussing a higher power is always difficult because we all carry our own mental model of what a god, or gods, or higher power is and does. These concepts are usually connected to each person's religious upbringing and culture. There are truly both some healthy and unhealthy religious concepts in most formal religions. A person can be religious but not spiritual. Any religion that excludes any group of people from its sense of compassion is not spiritual in my view. Religion tends to lose its spirituality when humility disappears and the need for competition and power creep in. I believe that Jesus, Buddha, Muhammad and other great religious leaders would not exclude anyone from their scope of compassion. Unfortunately, I know of some religious sects which are very conservatively insular do treat "outsiders" as inferior.

Reconciling religious tradition and spirituality is one of the cornerstones of the H.A.L.F. principles. My intent on focusing on these four ethics is to describe what can be a foundation for a spiritual life. I believe that these principles can lead to spirituality if we are all truly equal in terms of value on this earth. That value is the capacity to give and receive love. If we have that, then we are one loving spirit. That oneness must be non-material because we all have physical attributes that are somewhat unique. If we can appreciate those differences, each of us having equal value, what is left is the same shared pure loving energy.

I believe that living by these four ethics will help us easily live by the Serenity Prayer:

God, grant me the serenity to accept the things that I cannot change, the courage to change the things that I can, and the wisdom to know the difference.

We control our thinking and behavior and therefore our peace of mind when we live by these principles, providing that in our humility, we appreciate, love, and forgive ourselves and others equally and simultaneously. Those who follow these principles completely cannot exclude or try to control any group that doesn't follow them without transgressing the essential, basic acceptance of humility. If we are seeing others as of equal value, we are less likely to try to "correct" others to make them fit our own values.

Who Controls My Life?

Almost everything outside us is beyond our control. We never truly have *complete* control over another situation, event, or person. One of the major sources of anxiety and depression is the belief that situations and others control our lives by the power they have over us. In one of Dr. Wayne Dyer's self-help books, *You'll See It When You Believe It*, Dr. Dyer talks about the fact that we choose to see the world as a beautiful or ugly place. Where we allow our mind and behavior to go is where our emotions follow. We truly control our happiness by controlling our perception of how the world works. If we choose healthy thoughts and act on those thoughts, we have healthy emotions. We are clearly the captains of our own ships, that is, our souls. If we believe that other people can control us, then they can. This concept is easy to understand but often difficult to live by because of the distractions of old habits such as thinking and believing that other people, places, and events do take control of us.

Often I am confronted with a parent who asks the time-old question, "How do I control my kids?" Some time ago, a young couple came to my office for help disciplining their twin girls, who were acting out inappropriately. The girls refused to do anything that their parents requested no matter how much their parents yelled at them and threatened to punish them. In our discussions I noticed that the couple themselves fought regularly in a very loud manner. They told me that they drank to relax and admitted that they sometimes drank to excess, which didn't calm their tendency to argue. I pointed out to them that their lack of self-control was actually modeling irresponsible behavior for their children.

The parents agreed to stop arguing with each other and started calmly settling their differences without resorting to anger or bad temper. They reacted to their children's behavior by establishing appropriate logical consequences (e.g., setting a later bed-time as a reward for getting to bed on time other nights). Once they established this, their twin girls' behavior became more responsible.

The fact is, we don't control our kids. We guide them by how we control ourselves around them. By controlling ourselves around our children, we can give positive feedback and set up logical consequences for their behavior. We can set up an atmosphere where children want to be ethical and loving because they see that demonstrated in their own everyday experience. In short, rather than control our kids, we teach them by example. We also (if it is safe to do so) let consequences for choices that they make and actions that they take in the world teach our children and support them in dealing with those consequences.

The summer before Peter, my oldest son, started school, he picked up on my own very bad habit of cursing—not great modeling, I know, but it is what I did. I cautioned Peter that if he cursed in school, his teacher would punish him, perhaps by putting him in the corner facing the wall. The next day at school, he swore despite my sage advice. His teacher, unsurprisingly, sent him to the corner. Peter came home very indignant over the incident, telling me how unfair his teacher was for punishing him for something that I did all the time.; I pointed out the difference between home and school to him and commented that, given the circumstances, the teacher's action made sense to me. He pondered that and decided not to swear in school again. The onus was then on me to curb my own habit—at least when I was around the children.

It's easy to obsess over losing control. Feeling as if you have no control often drives depression, anxiety and low self-esteem. This past year, I had as a client a man whose obsession was that—should he die—he wouldn't be able to be there emotionally for his immediate family, a somewhat unusual obsession about the impossible. He was satisfied that his will and financial planning would take care of his family financially in the case of his demise, but that was not enough for him. He did learn to both meditate and exercise as ways to help control his anxiety, but, of course, those were palliatives and not solutions. Growing up in a family where everyone had well planned and successful lives, my client had known no major losses that interfered with his scheduled life. However, he had developed a expectation of resolute control over events in his life if he planned well and worked hard. Failure in this was not an option.

I encouraged him to think about many situations were choosing to let go of control brought good results: Surgical procedures where he had been healed only by giving up complete control over his bodily functions to a skilled surgeon, remembering a time when he was drowning and had to be saved by a life guard were two clear examples of the benefits of giving up control.

Through the counseling process and by having him explore some possible scenarios of what his death would look like to his family, he came to realize that his wife and children had a number of other family members and close friends who would be supportive of them. He also came to recognize that he was not alone. We all of have large parts of our lives that are beyond our control and that letting some things go can often be the most productive thing to do.

When we let things that are out of our control frustrate us, we usually find ourselves mired unproductive worry, a sign of momentary, bad mental health. Guiding our actions by the H.A.L.F.S. principles, puts us in command of the one thing we can control—ourselves and ultimately our mental health. We cannot, however, manage all the events in our lives such as eventual physical death, age, or the actions of other people. To be at peace, we must accept these events as out of our control. For many of us this is difficult; however, it is doable

Controlling our own thinking may be difficult—but it's crucial

Unless we are drugged, medicated, or blatantly psychotic, we control of our own thinking. Unfortunately, we often fall victim to patterns of thinking that have a way of becoming self-fulfilling prophesies. Habitual statements such as "I never win at anything" or "Women just don't like me" are things we may repeatedly say to ourselves inside our heads or even out loud, and little by little they become our reality. Quite frequently, when I suggest an alternative approach to a problem, clients insist, "I just don't think that way" or "I just don't feel that way." Often, we are so committed to our way of thinking that we don't even realize we have the agency to change it.

One woman came to me some time ago convinced that she was stupid and weak. We worked together for an extended period of time, and it came out that she had been exposed to a father and two ex-husbands who continually berated her in many ugly ways, convincing her that she was, indeed, both intellectually limited and emotionally ineffectual. She had internalized this view. In actuality, this woman had accomplished a number of difficult things. She had researched advanced treatments for her own cancer and successfully parented her daughter in spite of the great pain the cancer had brought her. We discussed where her self-assessment came from (in fact, of course, it was the assessment of others and not based on her actual experiences). After learning to listen to the voices of other, healthier, and more objective people around her, she was able to let go of the abusive opinions she had internalized and change her mindset. She divorced her latest abusive husband. Having become much more aware of where her negative thinking and resultant emotional problems actually came from, she recognized that she could truly change her thinking and attitude.

What this woman realized is something we all can do. We can willfully change our perspective, our habits of thinking, and our lives completely. If we are not aware of these habits or feel that they're immutable, these habits become who we are. With the help of those who love us and sympathetic others, we can control our reality, our lives in some ways, and our happiness. This happens much more easily if we are humble, appreciative, loving and forgiving. Our healthy relationships help us to change the quality of our lives by changing our thinking as it relates to others..

The serenity prayer, like so many profound ideas, is a simple concept that is at first hard to live by, but it works. In this prayer are encapsulated a major truth: mental health is about control and giving up control. We can make an impact, positive or negative, on the world by learning to manage our internal thoughts and feelings and by using that power to guide the way we interact with other people, recognizing that external events are often well beyond our control.

Our Bottom Line

I am a CNN news junkie. One of my favorite daily CNN programs is a show about saving money, "Your Bottom Line." While I do believe that this is a very important issue, I don't think it is the most critical issue in life. I draw the concept of a spiritual "bottom line" from this idea. I do believe that leading a humble, spiritual life, is the most important bottom line. When we live by the four ethics mentioned above, we are living a spiritual life, whether we see it or not, because we are in a loving relationship with people we meet.

We are able, sometimes through divine intervention, to see the world more spiritually. One morning, while I was writing, I had a moment of divine intervention. I noticed my 22-year-old cat,

Beebee, meowing in front of an elevated, open window next to my favorite chair. The day was beautiful, amazing, and the air was absolutely intoxicating. Beebee couldn't reach the window due to her arthritis. She was very happy when I lifted her up to the window sill to smell the spring air. I felt a rush of joy from being at one with her sensory pleasure. This was a spiritual moment for me. When I make spirituality my bottom line (and, unfortunately, I don't always do this), I frequently experience such joyful moments.

It is my view that it is wise to be a pragmatist (someone who does things that bring results). I think that, if our belief system does not bring peace of mind, then it's time to modify that system. I think we can choose to believe what we believe. When I view an experience such as the one that I had with Beebee as "divine intervention," my mental state is one of expansiveness, mental clarity, and pleasure. I chose to believe that my cat and I had a loving, spiritual connection. This is deeply practical for me. I pragmatically choose to believe this way because my entire day is more productive when I do.

Doing Nothing May Be Doing Something

I remember clearly a moment of spiritual intervention when I was rushing to get to my favorite AA meeting in Bedford, New Hampshire, near where I live. I sat down at the very large conference table, out of breath and irritated at being late. One of the men in the group that I was getting to know handed me a note that read: "It is far better to *be* a human *be*ing than to *be* a human *do*ing." I thought that was good advice. Clearly, it's important to get things done. It is even more important just to be quiet without external motion and be fully aware and at peace with our bodies, our surroundings, and our souls. It is better to be at peace than to be driven to produce, if our motive is to receive praise from others. We need to realize our goodness even when we're producing nothing tangible. To sit and listen to a friend in pain may be much more valuable than giving advice.

One of my personal issues is a tendency to sometimes rush and get agitated because I am not accomplishing enough. This is not spiritual, and I sometimes do things poorly because I rush. At the same time, while I am rushing, I'm doing nothing for my peace of mind. Many people sprint from one activity to the next with almost no quiet time in between. In short bursts, certainly, there is no harm in buzzing back and forth like a honeybee, but prolonged fits of relentless activity can be harmful. Exhaustion is a very real possibility, as is a loss of concentration and decreased quality of work. In some cases, like medical work or construction, loss of concentration through fatigue can pose risks to a person's own and other people's physical and emotional wellbeing. At times like these, it is important to stop and discipline oneself to be quiet and just be, even if it's only for a stolen moment.

Sometimes when we get a lot done but are not feeling spiritually connected, we end up feeling exhausted, restless, and empty. Once we practice being in the moment, being in touch with our inner and outer reality before beginning our task allows us to achieve fulfillment from the task itself. We then have better focus, control, and stamina; we might even finish a task more quickly. This means choosing to love our work rather than fearing imperfection and the judgment of others.

Corrupted Connection

I once had as a patient the parent of an adult child who had committed suicide. The child had had Asperger's syndrome (a communication disorder) and bi-polar disorder (a serious mood disorder). The father was devastated because he loved his son, but his son had always isolated himself so that he couldn't be reached. The younger man had been a brilliant organist and was well educated and employed, but at the age of 40 had never had a workable relationship with a significant other. He had few close friends and his music was never good enough for him to appreciate himself, in spite of the fact that others hearing him play enjoyed his music a great deal, He needed help liking himself because his two disorders made it difficult for him not to isolate from his loving family who could have supported his self-esteem. In a sense, it was partly his isolation that made him suicidal. People like this really don't love and appreciate themselves. They have lost or never found the joy of just-being. Efforts to achieve status often have out ranked quality relationships in importance. When people don't feel good about themselves, they are always running from failure, and this is very debilitating

To help the father over the distress he felt about his son's suicide—a good example of a situation which is ultimately beyond control, I reminded him of all the times that he and his wife had extended his life by taking him to a psychiatric hospital when it became obvious that he needed such help. We also worked together on helping him realize that, because their son had isolated himself, he and his wife were not privy to their son's mood immediately preceding his suicide and that his moods were, even with proper psychiatric care, at times unpredictable. While I believe that nothing can compensate for the pain of losing a child, my client did ultimately find some peace.

The epitome of unhappiness and poor mental health is suicide. During the suicidal ideation, a person in pain does not feel connected in a meaningful sense to people who should be significant in his or her life. Such people often feel that they haven't gotten enough done in their lives or, perhaps, that what they have accomplished isn't good enough. Efforts to achieve status often have outranked quality relationships in importance. When people don't feel good about themselves, they are always running from failure, and this is very debilitating.

In pain, the suicidal person may feel cut off from all their healthy connections. Often such a person makes statements such as "My family would be better off without me." He or she is not experiencing love of self or others because this person isn't viewing the value (appreciation) of himself or others around him. People in these straits find it difficult to express love for themselves or others due to depression, drug abuse, or mental illness. They need to know that any person's love for others always makes a difference, at least to the one doing the loving. *Acting* on the other three principles, Humility, Appreciation, and Forgiveness, can work together to help people keep their connections with others loving. Except for some chemical imbalance, a suicidal ideation tends to slip away once a person experiences this loving connection.

Even though the various religions of the world including Islam, Hinduism, Buddhism, Christianity, and Judaism have been valuable sources of sound mental health, often the basic tenants of these major religions get lost in their institutionalization. A good example of this is the idea of eternal damnation by a Christian God. Logically, no God can be both all forgiving and at the same time punishing the same person for eternity. Because of this contradiction, I see clients who feel guilty about a mistake that, they believe, God could never forgive.

One woman with whom I worked had had an abortion during the time when she was an active alcoholic. Having been raised in a religiously conservative Christian family, she had been taught that abortion was a sin so heinous that it was unforgivable. Convinced that she was eternally damned, she was distraught. While I am not a minister or a priest, to relieve her anguish, together we explored the power of forgiveness that lies at the core of most Christian belief and the lessons that Jesus himself taught about it. Once she could recognize that the rigid approach that her family affixed to sin was in fact not the essential teaching of her Church, her confliction about her situation resolved itself.

Eternal damnation is a concept that clearly produces poor mental health. When formalized religion loses its humility and discourages rational thought, a seriously corrupted connection within us and between ourselves and others develops. This corrupted connection can create great damage to our mental health and, at times, encourage suicide. The priority in our search for good mental health is a loving relationship with ourselves and others. Any religion or philosophy that does not foster loving relationships should be discarded.

CHAPTER II: STRAIGHT LINES AND CIRCLES

One of the biggest barriers to mental health is that our goal-oriented nature can become an obsession in our daily lives. We get burnt out, anxious, and depressed. If our days are *only* about getting certain things done, meditation, rest, recreation, and fun don't play an important part of in our quest to have a good day.

This approach becomes a hidden program for disaster. I should talk. I am still struggling with this way of thinking. I get involved in getting the dishes done, walking the dog, scheduling my clients, answering phone calls, etc. to the point where I'm running out of gas. I'm not suggesting that procrastination is the answer either. I am saying that if we do not stay alert to our physical and emotional needs, *while* we are getting things done, we get discouraged and give up. If, on the other hand, we focus frequently on our relationships with others and our own wellbeing, we have more energy to do a better job with the various linear goals that we have such as building a business or getting a higher educational degree.

In nature, energy moves in circles; rest brings energy; the use of energy brings rest. The energy of our lives also works in circles. We exert energy to work out and stay healthy; to work on our careers to earn money; and to bring up our children and/or care for the other important people in our lives. We hopefully have the energy to do all this well. If we give equal importance to recreation, rest, and physical and emotional nurturance for ourselves, we will have the energy to continue to do this. The not doing must be as important as the doing.

This *exertion* of energy comes naturally to most of us as we're getting things done. However, we are far less conscious of the energy that comes in; what sort is coming in; how much of it we get in the form of advice and encouragement (or, in a negative situation discouragement) from friends and family or even from the internet;, where it's coming from and our attitude toward receiving that incoming energy. As hard working, high-achieving Americans, we tend to forget *how* and *from what source* we get our energy. It is very easy to undervalue rest and being receptive. This is a mistake that can lead to exhaustion, anxiety, and depression.

We can simply gulp down a meal or feverishly consume sensual experiences – sex, sweets, or even stimulants—without appreciating their pleasures. On the other hand, we could savor these experiences, be grateful for them, and be careful of how much we take in and the consequences of taking them in. Receiving the good things in life *appreciatively* gives us a lot of energy to make us more productive.

Life at its best is a smooth giving and receiving of good, purposeful energy. For example, I have learned that my trying to be perfect is a hindrance to being a good therapist. Being open about my mistakes helps a client bond with me more easily. I also have learned that some people really don't want much of any input but that they grow psychologically just from empathetic listening. Over the years I've learned these lessons far better from my clients than from what I got in graduate school. A good therapy session becomes a back-and-forth exchange of energy. There is teaching and learning on the part of my clients but also for me. It is different from other relationships in that my clients are paying me for giving them an attentive, listening ear, guidance in rethinking their problems, and at times just plain advice. However, I am also getting feedback on how effective my approach is, and I am being exposed to knowledge that I might not have about experiences that I have never had. *Appreciating* what I am taking in gives me energy.

This circle of relationships has benefitted both of us. If, on the other hand, I simply talk about the material from my notes from the previous session and am very mindful of the 50-minute hour passing, I may complete my goal of covering the necessary therapeutic material, but my clients may feel as alone with their problems as when they walked in. Furthermore, I am getting tired and wanting to go home. The quality of the connection between us is extremely important.

If I am savoring the magic of the communication and aware of my clients' and my own joy in enriching each others' lives, I feel uplifted and successful. I get and appreciate a strong feeling of purpose and joy from our interaction. I try to express my gratitude, not just for being paid for my services but from the sense of meaning and spiritual satisfaction that I have received from my interaction with a client. I am, of course, grateful for being paid for my services;

however, the monetary gain for that therapeutic hour is only one part of my gain.

In the type of relationship (psychotherapy) that I've described above, the process of relating carries as much importance as the therapeutic problem. The task of helping my clients to reduce their anxiety and depression is *linear*; i.e., I am encouraging a change in behavior which helps people go from greater anxiety and depression to less. Relationship communication is, for better or worse, a circle of both talking and listening. This is often accomplished by giving my clients the assignment to rethink a problematic situation and change certain behaviors. What makes the assigning of this homework and the reinforcement for completing its work is the relationship between a client and me. That is the *circular* process, speaking and listening attentively on both of our parts. It is a give and take between us.

In all my professional work, if my client and I are both in a *humble* state (one of mutual respect), there is mutual appreciation. It is the circle of giving generously and receiving with gratitude that makes us both truly happy. If I am appreciative or grateful for what I have received in the interaction, the circle of energy is far more productive. Sometimes I may end up with more energy than when the interaction began. Gratitude (or *appreciation*) is like a catalyst that helps produce energy while energy is being spent.

In our culture we tend to be obsessed with linear, task-oriented thinking and behavior. The problem is that, by attaining one linear goal after another (a bachelor's degree followed by a master's degree, followed a PhD, or several promotions in succession at work) does not bring the kind of satisfaction that living by the H.A.L.F.S. can. Linear achievements can enrich our lives if living by the H.A.L.F.S. principles is the priority. The linear achievements lose their meaning if the quality of our relationships is not progressively improving while we are attaining them. As a matter of fact, I have seen people who achieve little in the way of status become rapidly more enthusiastic about their lives once the intimacy of their relationships begins to improve. A client I'll call Fred, one of my more artistic clients, makes jewelry for a living but does not make a lot of money. His financial situation put a strain on his marriage. However, when he and his wife improved their overall communication, their financial situation was still a struggle, but usually they were very happy just to love each other fully. Their financial situation was easily faced by two cooperative fully functioning people. The title of this book, *Nice People Finish First*, refers to the concept that, when we are kind to others (nice to them) and equally kind to ourselves, we reach a state of self-satisfaction much more quickly than those people whose lives are simply about achieving.

It's important to remember that to be emotionally healthy, being kind (nice) to others always necessitates being as kind to ourselves. If, in achieving our linear goal of more education, greater financial security, and the like, we prioritize being kind, we will feel happy even before the linear goal has been reached. Having satisfying relationships while goal seeking, demands a smooth circle of giving and taking. What we finish or achieve that makes us truly happy is a smooth creative circle of giving to and receiving from others and ourselves. This is true happiness.

The circle of giving and receiving within ourselves fuels and guides what we can do with others. It comes from an internal dialogue and the behaviors we adopt to make ourselves healthier. When, for example, we work out and exert ourselves, our bodies release fatigue toxins and we receive increased norepinephrine, dopamine, and oxygen. While this increases our sense of well-being, it also gives whatever personal communication we send to others increased clarity and enthusiasm. The *inner* circle of giving and receiving (treating ourselves in a loving manner) is the core of the ability to give to and receive from others. If I can be humble within myself, realizing that I am equal to everyone else as a valuable human being and I appreciate my value, I will be inclined to do loving things for my mental and physical health and forgive myself for my failures. I can then have the same enriched circle of energy exchange with others. Throughout the following pages, it is important to thoroughly understand that the most important goal is reaching a state of being involved in this ongoing healthy circle of giving and receiving both within oneself and with others. While we are actively participating in this circle of giving and receiving, the goal of happiness is often attained *instantly* and throughout our lives. The "nice person" reaches the goal of happiness first. The goal is the process of having healthy relationships.

CHAPTER III: HUMILITY

Humility is the foundation and the fulcrum or balancing point of sound mental health. Humility prevents our becoming arrogant or self-loathing. Humility is a perception of our individual selves as a piece of a larger jigsaw puzzle; in creating the whole picture, *each of us as pieces are <u>unique</u> but no one piece is more important than the other*. This whole picture is of a world that is both beautiful and highly efficient.

Humility, appreciation, love, and forgiveness tend to work in a circle. When we are humble, we tend to appreciate, love, and forgive others and ourselves. We recognize our need for these things. Humility bestows balance and helps connect us to one another in a healthy manner. We become united with those around us.

The Power of Humility

Humility is power. This may seem like a strange statement. However, if you think of humility as a channel to give and receive energy this statement makes sense. If I am humble then I take in all the information that is coming in to me unfiltered by prejudice or ignorance. If I am arrogant, I may well ignore advice that may be very helpful. If I see myself as of little value (self-deprecating) then I may be too anxious or shy to give full attention to what is being said. Here's a simple example of what I mean.

Many years ago when my eight-year-old daughter, Gretchen, said to me, "Daddy, I know why people take drugs and drink too much. They don't feel loved," I didn't really listen or fully appreciate what she was saying. She was my young daughter, and I was a trained psychologist who didn't need advice from a child. I didn't immediately see the intrinsic value of her observation. However, once I did take it in, that simple but profound truth gave me a new perspective that is highly useful whenever I am working professionally with an addict. I initially just viewed it as a cute thing for my daughter to say. Had I been more humble, perhaps that truth would have appeared with more clarity far earlier than it did, and I would have been more helpful to my clients. I wasn't being humble, so I missed out on her wisdom at that time.

There's another side to inadequate humility—a lack of self-esteem. People often don't see a lack of self-esteem as a lack of humility. I do. My son's godfather, Joe, retired at an early age. His very successful career as a financial planner made that possible. However, whenever the issue of finances would come up, I didn't fully listen to his advice because the whole field of financial planning made me ashamed of how poorly I had planned my own finances. Lacking self-esteem, I didn't see myself as equal to Joe, and the consequence was poor communication. Joe was saying the right things in the right way, but I was unable to complete the circle by hearing what he had to say. Had I been able to maintain a measure of humility (i.e., seen myself as equally intelligent), I might have listened more closely to Joe's advice, followed it, and saved myself a great deal of money. But I didn't want to admit my ignorance about financial matters.

Humility is A Guide to Giving and Receiving

Humility also can govern the quality of what we give and receive. If we see that what we have to give is of equal importance to what others (who have greater gifts in a particular area) have to give, we tend to give more. When my mother was 87 before she died at 88, she often felt that she had nothing much to give. She lived in a fine assisted-living facility where all her physical needs were not only met but often anticipated. When Mom commented that she had little to give, I told her that I was still learning from her. Her grace in dealing with her failing faculties (physical movement, memory, etc.) was a lesson to me in how to deal with the aging process. I told my Mom that she also offered words of wisdom, advice, and stories from her vast life experiences that taught me a lot and that I appreciated.

Before she died, Mom gave me her 2000 Buick LeSabre with only 43,000 miles on it because she could no longer drive. At the time my car was beginning to fall apart, so I was very grateful. When she humbly asked if I wanted her "old" car, I gratefully accepted with a good deal of enthusiasm. She realized (with some helpful input from my brother) that this was a possession that had value to someone, me. While it is true that Mom's advice and loving concern were far more important than the gift of a nice car, this was a gift that I was humble enough to receive (recognizing that I needed a car) and mom appreciating that she indeed had something she could give, despite her age. To me and to Mom, the car was a symbol of love.

Arrogance

Of course, arrogance is obviously a lack of humility. A client of mine, a successful businessman, came to me with a problem. He couldn't get close to his wife and five-year-old daughter. He was, however, very proud of his 2 new sports cars, which, for him, symbolized his worth as a person, and this led him to arrogance.

One of the events we discussed involved him and his young daughter. She had spilled breakfast cereal on the back seat of his new BMW, and my client reacted with fury. He lost his temper with his little girl. His outburst was just the sort of thing that widened the emotional distance between the two. However, to my client's credit, he saw his reaction as a problem and was seeking help for it. At the time of the incident, however, his daughter's feelings were clearly less important to him than his prized possession. When he accepted this and recognized it as the kind of thing that drove a wedge between him and his family, he began to act with humility. He focused more on his daughter's feelings and overcame the distance between them. He likewise started to have a more intimate relationship with his wife, who had been very discouraged by my client's obsession with neatness and the need for things to be perfect. He began to actually make his wife's feelings a priority, and she returned the favor.

A curious thing I've discovered is that it is usually my wealthiest of clients who make it difficult to collect payment on what they owe me. I often hear about such clients' expensive vacations or the toys that they are proud of, but they don't seem to notice that they have a significant outstanding balance with my office. Conversely, the people who struggle most financially are often the ones most motivated to pay their bill as quickly as possible. Those who struggle seem to know what it means not to be paid well for their hard work.

Humility was clearly the state of mind of the founders of the major religions of the world. Jesus, Mohamed, and the Buddha along with humble practitioners such as Gandhi were all in the habit of sitting on the ground to talk to the people who were willing to listen. These great leaders were not concerned with political power, they were more concerned about teaching humility. Humility was their power, and people wanted to listen.

Many times when I have needed something, being humble has helped me get my needs met. Recently, I walked out of my condo building into the rain. Focused on snatching the new bottle of laundry soap, I forgot my keys. I was frustrated but managed to calm down. A car pulled into the parking lot by my building. While I didn't recognize the driver or passenger, I saw myself with a bottle of laundry soap in my hands, soaked to the skin and realized that I obviously looked like someone in distress. Given that, I didn't think that I would be viewed as a threat, so I flagged down the car and, explaining that I'd forgotten my keys, asked them to please open the building door, which they promptly did. Had I been too focused on myself as a self-sufficient adult and too proud to ask for help, I might still be out in the rain. It certainly would have taken much longer to get inside, and I probably would have been late for work. I needed help and I'm glad that I wasn't too proud to ask for it.

Being Humble About Making Plans and Setting Goals

The *Myers-Briggs* psychological test breaks people down into broad personality categories. One of the personalities is the "J-type," a person who has a need to be goal-oriented and likes to make plans. That's me.

Being a J-type has worked well for me at times, when, for example, I wanted to start a family or plan a career in psychology. While I reached those goals, others eluded me. Had I not been able at times to be humble when confronted with the frustration of not getting something I wanted, I probably never would have been able to reset my goals and move forward. When I was a very young man, these kinds of goal resets were very stressful for me. At times, when I am not being mindful, they can still be a challenge for me. However, resetting goals and changing plans are not necessarily bad things. They can lead to some unexpected benefits.

I did not set out to have a career in psychology. I wanted to be a Methodist minister. Giving up on my initial goal was a huge reset. Here's what happened.

I had completed my undergraduate double major in religion and philosophy at American University to prepare for the Wesley Seminary in Washington, DC. I even had the good fortune as a preministerial student to obtain a position as a part-time director of religious education at St. Luke's Methodist Church in northwest

D.C. I was all set for my chosen career. Everything was planned, and I could see reaching the goal, almost to touch it.

Little did I know that gross hypocrisy and racial discrimination in the church where I was working would smack me in the face and change my life. That congregation's hypocrisy turned me away from organized religion completely. The most glaring act of hypocrisy occurred when the ushers escorted a Black family out of the church one Sunday. When I inquired about the incident, the senior pastor said, "We don't want our congregation to be uncomfortable; we had no choice." This was traumatic, shaking my belief system to the core. Totally disillusioned, I decided that I wanted no part of organized religion, but I didn't know where to turn. I looked for career guidance from the American University counseling office.

I took aptitude, intelligence, and personality tests to get some sense of direction for a different career. I needed to satisfy my desire to help others in a venue that made sense. This evaluation pointed me in the direction of psychology, and I began to plan my new career enthusiastically.

I have been blessed. I've had a rewarding career that, so far, has lasted more than 50 years. Because of my exposure to gross hypocrisy while working in that local church, I had to reset my goal to find a meaningful direction for my professional life. In order to emotionally adjust to this radical turn of events, I had to be humble enough to accept that sometimes my efforts for achieving some goals went in the wrong direction and to move on.

Humility as a Source of Power

Dr. Emery Varhely, my supervisor at the New York State Drug Addiction Control Commission Rehab Center in New York City, was among the most powerful men I've ever met. That doesn't mean that he controlled the fate of nations or some such; his power came from one of his major personality traits – his humility. When I was working at the Rehab Center, we got word that we could choose a new chairman of our department from among the applicants. Dr. Varhely's resume impressed us all. He held three master's degrees in various fields, a PhD in clinical psychology, and extensive experience in the field. We set up an interview with him with the approval of the director of the rehab center for the next week.

When we met Dr. Varhely for the first time, we found that he was a gentle, friendly man who seemed to love people in general. We were in awe of him and his credentials, so we were somewhat taken aback when he told us that, rather than refer to him as Dr. Varhely, we should call him Emery. As he talked to our group, this humble man reminded us often to use his first name rather than his title. I always listened to him intensely both because I respected his expertise and because he had a friendly, humble nature.

The rehab center was somewhat of a maximum-security institution, because some of the drug addicts in treatment were felons. There was a narcotics rehab officer for every 25 men, and the facility was run like a prison. Emery often walked into the 25-man units to talk with the men. He always suggested to the men in treatment that they call him by his first name, and his friendly demeanor never differed whether he was talking to the staff or to the men in residence. The residents also respected him and felt incredibly comfortable with him. Emery didn't care whether an individual had been involved in armed robbery or had a clean legal record; they were all important to him, and he was dedicated to their recovery.

Emery once told me about a scary incident that occurred while he was working in a prison in another state. Talking to the inmates, he was stabbed by an angry man who apparently hated everyone. Emery recuperated in the hospital, and the the facility placed his attacker in solitary confinement. Weeks later, Emery went walking on the unit where he had been stabbed, and the inmates gave him a standing ovation. Emery missed talking to the inmates face to face. He respected them, and they respected him. That's real power.

The 1984 film, *The Karate Kid*, exemplifies how I see humility. In the film Daniel Russo, the young main character, is forced to move from New Jersey to Los Angles. As the new kid in an unfamiliar environment, he faced bullying from some students of a karate dojo that taught its students to be merciless bullies. Wanting to fight back, Daniel learns from his mentor, Mr. Miyagi, that balance is more important than aggression to win in his. By developing emotional balance, the young hero goes from being intimidated by his tormentors to being confident. Mr. Miyagi teaches Daniel traditional Okinawan Karate, a defensive martial art never to be used for aggression. The young man also learns to be humble about his new skills.

Daniel later competes for a trophy to gain the respect of the bullies and wins the contest in self-defense against one of the bullies in a controlled setting. By handling the situation this way, he demonstrates that his non-violent philosophy makes it possible to stand tall and foster mutual respect among those who would harm him.

Humility creates balance. We care for ourselves and others equally. Without humility there is no balance. Without humility; arrogance or self-hatred can easily develop. In either case we find ourselves isolated from people and situations that could help us develop and stay emotionally sound.

Humility is *Not* Low Self-Esteem

People often see the word *humility* but hear *low self-esteem*. This is a common misunderstanding. In this book, humility means seeing ourselves as being of equal value to those around us. Humility helps us receive with gratitude and give with generosity. This balanced giving and receiving is imperative for those who would be vibrant, fully functioning people.

Humility is the slippery bedrock of the other principles of mental health. It's the bedrock because when we remain truly humble is it possible to connect with others, hear what they have to say, and absorb their thoughts into our own in a creative way and hopefully arrive at something deeper and further developed. This is possible because I assign an equal value to both the ideas of others and my own. The bedrock is slippery because it's hard to stay balanced between the extremes of narcissism (or being self-centered) and codependence (loving others but not ourselves).

Humility and Religion

It is my belief that Humility is a central value in the beginning stages of many religions. Unfortunately, that value has frequently been weakened or lost favor in the development of religious institutions over time. The human quest for power over others has often overwhelmed the humility of many of the early religious principles.

The early Christians had no church buildings; the followers were considered the "church." As time marched on, church buildings became cathedrals, and a mammoth hierarchy of power developed. Too often, religious people no longer saw each other as equals. There developed a hierarchy of priests, bishops, archbishops and, in Roman Catholicism, a pope. Humility in the sense of the equality of human value got lost. However, the most recent pope, Pope Francis, has made great strides in setting an example of humility. While time will tell what Francis's influence will mean in the long term, the example of humility will not be easy to maintain after centuries of the rigid power structure within the Catholic Church. I find this most unfortunate because the quality of love and care for each other has its foundation in humility.

My Friend, the Atheist

Dr. Ronald Goldberg was a psychologist who worked in my hometown of Derry, NH. A very bright man, he worked with me at the New Hampshire State Hospital. Ron's political views about the treatment of the adolescent patients who we both worked with were completely opposite to mine. We often had intense arguments over how the administration was handling treatment at the hospital. We kept our distance from each other personally: our therapeutic approaches differed, our philosophies differed, and our religious understandings differed. We had, I thought at the time, literally nothing in common. I was wrong.

When we both left the hospital and started our own private practices in Derry, we very gradually got to know each other in a different context. From community feedback, I began to recognize that Ron was an excellent psychotherapist who cared deeply about his clients. We became friends.

One day, Ron asked whether he could be a part of my weekly peer consultation group where I met with my staff at Derry Counseling Service. He explained that he had a brain tumor and wanted to be closely associated with other professionals who could give him honest feedback about his competence as a therapist. His doctors were uncertain as to whether or not this tumor would affect his ability to be a good psychologist. Ron hoped to use the group's observations to measure the effect of his brain tumor on his work. His humility touched me. I admired his courage and told him he would be a welcome addition to our group.

Each week, he asked for feedback about his ability to

practice. The group agreed that Ron was behaving appropriately with his clients. Eventually, however, he was dissatisfied with how he had handled one case and decided to surrender his license, but he asked to continue meeting with the other therapists and me to have some intellectual stimulation. The group agreed that Ron's input on cases would be an asset to us, and we looked forward to giving him emotional support.

As Ron's cancer progressed, he and I grew closer. We began to appreciate each other in our common goal of helping our clients. Ron was an atheist; I was a strong believer in a God. Both of us, however, enjoyed helping people have richer lives and that gave us common ground apart from our religious differences.

I began grieving Ron's loss of health and started visiting him at home. He couldn't drive any longer, and walking any distance was simply impossible. Unbeknownst to me, but Ron asked his wife to approach me to direct the funeral service for him. Ron passed away a few months later in January of 1998. In 1998, as a psychologist I was still very different from Ron. He was a true scholar and very knowledgeable of the latest research in the field. He was probably much more of a social scientist than I. I am now and was then more of an eclectic, more of a philosophical practitioner than Ron. He was a more of a left brain, linear thinker than I was, more empirical in his thinking and much more detail oriented. My approach to psychotherapy has always been a mixture of philosophical and empirical (research oriented) thinking. I believe that in seeing each other as equals (attempting to be humble), we learned from one another. I was, I believe, good at more abstract thinking about therapeutic problems, but Ron's vast knowledge of psychological research was truly helpful to me.

When it came to some of my religious concepts, Ron was good at making me be more thoroughly logical in my conclusions about religious matters. He was a humanitarian; I was a spiritual philosopher. Ron helped make my philosophical and religious thinking more practical. I was more expressive of my emotions; Ron was very much like *Star Trek*'s Dr. Spock, highly intellectualized. What brought us together was our fascination with and love of people. I believe that God was pleased with our relationship.

When Marlene, Ron's wife, told me that Ron had wanted me

to direct his funeral service, I was both shocked and touched, honored that he Ron also requested that there be no mention of God in this service Because he didn't believe in God, Ron wanted no mention of him in the service. One thought occurred to me then, as it does now as I write this: I'm certain that God believed in Ron. He had led the life of a kind-hearted healer and, surely, in this and many other ways, a spiritual life irrespective of his atheism.

My background and beliefs made me struggle to leave God out of Ron's memorial service. Nonetheless, I asked for God's help as I fulfilled his request. I firmly believed that God was in Ron's life and had guided his actions even if Ron himself didn't recognize this. I believe that God is a part of all our loving thoughts and actions, whether we are aware of this or not. To me, a humble, love-centered life *is* a God-centered life because God is the universal spirit of love. In some ways, I realized that I didn't have to struggle with semantics to direct the funeral service. I knew in my heart that talking about Ron's loving work with his clients and his loving relationships with his family and friends *was* very much including God in the service without using that word.

The love that Ron expressed in his life represented the God that I believe in. It is the God of a people whether they are Christian, Jew, Muslim, Hindu, Buddhist or atheist. It is the God that believes in us when we don't believe in Him. God is love and Ron was a loving person, whether he chose to use the word *God* or not. During the service, people talked about Ron's kind and generous acts. They talked about his unique manner of caring for others. At the conclusion of the service, I felt convinced that his influence would be eternal and therefore his life would be eternal.

All of life is energy. To optimize our positive energy, we must be humble in the sense that we need to receive with gratitude as we give with generosity. Like the negative and positive poles on a battery, this circle is the Yin and Yang of life. In Taoist philosophy, the Yin is receptive and the Yang is a more assertive force. It is the Taoist belief that they naturally work together in perfect harmony. If we are truly humble, we realize that we need to value the reception of good things as much as we value our giving. When we do this, we are balanced and indeed emotionally healthy.

Unfortunately, in our achievement-oriented culture keeping

in balance what we give and what we receive is not perceived as being goal oriented. If I use linear thinking (i.e., a goal directed approach to life) exclusively or am committed to the ultimate importance of tangible tokens of achievement (e.g., a better income, more education, a position of power), the idea of living in this balanced circle has less appeal. As a result, my life could easily begin to lose the balance between receiving with gratitude and giving with generosity. I could get drained of energy and easily become depressed.

Arrogance and Poor Self-Esteem

Arrogance – one form of inadequate humility – leads to unnecessary criticism of others and denial of our own shortcomings. The arrogant person becomes blocked from true intimacy and ends up isolated without a sufficient support system. The growth that could occur by facing our own shortcomings doesn't occur because of denial. Arrogant people develop a distorted view of the world and sees themselves as different and alone.

Poor self-esteem, the opposite of arrogance, is the other form of inadequate humility. It likewise leads to isolation through poor connections with others and a lack of inner harmony. People with poor self-esteem tend to disbelieve the complements they receive and sometimes might feel that the complement is either sarcasm or a poor attempt to be polite. Such a person often doesn't allow the positive feedback be received and internalized.

I've already noted this, but it is a concept that bears repeating: humility is the grounding for all mental health. This bedrock is slippery because of the balancing act that we work at to remain humble is difficult. We cannot afford to be either self-effacing or arrogant. We need to feel of equal importance to all those around us. Sometimes we can swing from arrogance to self-deprecation. This swinging from one extreme to the other is very noticeable in active substance abusers. The tendency is also clear with immature individuals and young people. However, I see this propensity to some degree in all people (including myself). In a humble state, our communication with others, particularly if they are humble, can be very gratifying.

Many years ago I had a conversation with an older man, whom I had never met, in the steam room at my health club. We were both naked and relaxing after hard workouts. We talked about our love of working out and our families. Not having my contact lenses in, I didn't notice whom I was talking to. He was, in fact, Pat Buchanan, a candidate for President of the United States at that time. After putting my contacts in, I saw secret service people around the locker room. We had begun to know each other as people sharing a common world, even though he was running on a ticket for a political party that was not mine and was far more conservative than I. The two of us bonded briefly in a number of areas and began to like each other's company. For me, it was a real lesson in humility. I'll have to admit that I wouldn't have been so relaxed and open if I'd known the status of the person I was talking to. Naked in the steam room, there were no indications of superior and inferior status. Not having my contact lenses in helped me avoid focusing on our differences.

Giving and Not Receiving

If we are truly humble, we realize that, like those around us, *we need* appreciation, love, and forgiveness as much as our fellow humans. Many of the people that I have worked with as a psychotherapist are ready to appreciate, love, and forgive others but despise themselves for not being good enough. In a subconscious or conscious attempt not to appear self-centered, they ignore their own emotional needs. The vast majority of my clients fall into this category. They come in depressed and/or very anxious because they cannot meet the needs of those that they care about. They appreciate, love, and forgive others but not themselves. Often, they develop physical health problems as well due to stress and toxic emotions. Susan, one of my clients who had been working for children's protective services, was very hard working and empathetic with the children who made up her caseload. However, she often came home exhausted physically and emotionally drained. As a result, she became very short tempered with her own children as well as with her husband. She needed more time away from work when she could rest and have fun with her family and recreational activities for herself. At the time she was seeing me for therapy, she had had to resign her position. Eventually she got a job that wasn't so demanding and learned to get recreation and take time to rest. She – and her family – were much happier.

Arrogant people that I've met usually don't come into a

psychotherapist's office because they see themselves as islands unto themselves, unconnected to others in any intimate manner. They are often more interested in their finances, power, and expensive toys than intimacy. They can easily become addicted to more material things or in some cases to substance abuse to fill the emptiness of poor emotional intimacy. Unfortunately, such fixes are very temporary.

People with poor self-esteem may also lack emotional intimacy because they may abuse substances or have other obsessions to fill the emptiness inside. True humility allows emotional intimacy on a large scale, reducing anxiety and depression in a healthy manner. The arrogant feel that they don't need others and those with poor self-esteem often feel that others don't need them. In either case, the emotional intimacy is damaged. *Emotional intimacy is the deep healthy, creative connection that keeps us mentally and psychologically sound.*

Being a psychologist, I have the advantage of knowing that people need me. I know this because my clients make appointments and the insurance companies pay for my time with them. I have my professional credentials to help me feel that I can make a difference in my own manner. However, I must always be willing to accept advice and care from others who have their own expertise or from family and friends who want to give me love and support. Mental health professionals can very easily get wrapped up in supporting others and not receiving the same support themselves. This can be a recipe for disaster.

In the winter of 2006, I fell on the ice in front of my office building. I completely severed the tendon in my quadriceps. This occurred at the same time that I was being treated for three bulging discs in my lower back. Needless to say, I missed some work due to my inability to walk and the severe pain I was experiencing. I couldn't work out at the health club or practice with my church choir. These were activities that I relied on to socialize. Radically cut off from much of my social contacts, I got quite depressed. Once again, I realized that I needed people – people to help me medically, people to help me do things I couldn't do because of my handicap, and people to socialize with. Once I realized this, I got some counseling for myself and reached out to my friends. Once I did this

– accessing the help of others, I soon felt much better.

If I keep my attitude clear, being a psychotherapist is a great vehicle for energy balance. My clients pay for my professional interaction with them; however, they give back to me in other ways as well. They give me ideas, stimulation, and purpose. I learn a great deal from them. I also derive a great deal of satisfaction from being able to assist them to function better.

Particularly in my private life, humility allows me to learn as I teach, to give and receive affection. Sending and receiving affection are equally important. I definitely do *not* believe that "it is more blessed to give than to receive." Giving, to me, is of equal importance as receiving, if receiving is done with appreciation or gratitude. As we receive with gratitude, we have more to give to others (and, we can hope, do so with a more generous attitude); the circle of life is complete. If people who receive our gratitude are grateful, *they* have more to give. We are creating energy as we take it in.

Dealing with Great Loss

On March 18, 2008, I lost my 23-year-old son, Nick. He died

very suddenly and unexpectedly. With the traumatic shock came pain that I had never experienced before and hope never to experience again. No death can be more profoundly shaking than the death of a child.

Nick was charismatic. He was 6'4", had blue eyes, blond curly hair, and a body builder's physique. He was very handsome and for a while we were preparing him to be a male model until his interest in that waned. He had been in superb physical condition. His blues eyes sparkled with humor, intelligence, and intensity. His Christopher Waken imitation could split your sides. Nick was intensely passionate and articulate. When he cried, he would sob. When Nick laughed, he could electrify a room. At times he could be intensely angry (and more than a little scary to people who didn't know him). He could also be as tender as a new mother with a child. His physical, emotional and intellectual energy could attract or at times command a whole room, even when he was silent. I loved Nick as much as I could have loved anyone. The week before he died, he told me that I was a good dad, and I was overwhelmed.

Nick died two blocks from our home. He died from an

interaction of Valium, which he took for anxiety, and the alcohol in the beer he drank at a party on an empty stomach. I was ripped apart emotionally. My whole world was distorted and black. There was nothing else in my consciousness of significance. All of a sudden, I was a different person.

Grief over the loss of my son still lingers, but the pain is not as crippling. What helped my tortured soul most and enabled me to begin to pull out of the blackest of holes was being receptive at his funeral and later on to the support people offered. I allowed myself to be receptive to hundreds of people who cared about Nick and our family. I realized that I needed to be an open vessel.

As I looked out from the pulpit of the church during his funeral service, I tried (without much success) to talk about Nick. I welled up and couldn't speak. However, I could feel the overwhelming power of love and empathy in the eyes of my friends and family in the congregation. My older son, Peter, took over and read what I had written. I honestly felt God's love filling me up through the channel of those faces and the gaze of their eyes as I stood in the pulpit of our church.

I still miss my son Nick a great deal, but what has kept my grief from crippling my life has been my willingness to be humble enough to realize that I need to appreciate the love that surrounds me from my immediate family, friends and the higher power I believe in. I know that Nick and my higher power forgave the mistakes that I made with him as his father. I need to also be humble enough to appreciate, love and forgive myself for the mistakes that I made. My healing is all based on humility. I was the healer who needed healing. Those of us who love and forgive need to be loved and forgiven to thrive.

Contrasting Mediocrity and Balance

We are a nation of extremes. Too many of us dread the idea of being mediocre. *Living a balanced life and remaining as humble as possible is without question a difficult task.* It takes constant vigilance (and hard work) to remain balanced as we work at being humble. A balanced life, however, is not a mediocre one. For those who live in humility, this attitude is like a perpetual energy machine, taking in what we need and giving out what others need. In this state we connect with others in a healthy, creative manner.

Denial and Projection

Denial and projection are two unconscious defense mechanisms that make being humble a difficult task. With denial we block out our own negative traits subconsciously when we are too ashamed to face the shortcomings that we have. When we use projection, which fits neatly with denial, we see our own negative traits in others. An unfortunately too common example of this is individuals or groups who become aggressive or violent in the name of peace. Anger seems to be one of those emotions that it is far easier to see in others than in ourselves.

In the early 1970s The Weathermen, a faction of the SDS (Students for a Democratic Society), a group who advocated and demonstrated for peace, were at times very violent. This is a prime example of denial and projection. The Weathermen had an important thing to say regarding the terrible violence and loss of life that occurred during the Vietnam War. This radical faction didn't seem to grasp the tragic error in harming innocent people when they set off bombs in the American Capital to communicate and gain attention for their concerns for the end of violence.

CHAPTER IV: APPRECIATION

When we appreciate someone or something, we see the value within ourselves and others or the external value (such as a beautiful painting), and we have a sense of enrichment and pleasure. With something like the Grand Canyon, appreciation appears to be a nearly automatic process. But sometimes appreciation is a choice. A person can choose to see the beauty in an old tree, for example, when perceived as a whole or, in contrast, the imperfections or poor symmetry in the same tree. Appreciation also frequently involves valuing ourselves or others as whole beings in spite of the imperfections of either.

There is an old psychological rule that states that *perception is selective*. We are often governed in our perceptions of the world by our emotional state at the time of perception; if we are in a positive state of mind, we are more predisposed to see things positively and vice versa. We can overcome our tendency to perceive negatively by looking for the value inside ourselves and around us. We can redirect our attitude by choosing what we will emphasize in our perception. Is the glass empty or half full?

By nature, I am a restless soul, and become easily grumpy if I cannot control things like my painful arthritis. However, I can improve my mood when I command myself to "Be grateful." Grateful for what? For me, the what includes that I thoroughly enjoy my career, at age 77, have people who love me just as I am, and am generally in good health gives me reasons for feeling grateful. Once I focus there, I stop feeling grumpy and experience satisfaction.

If I have had little sleep and my very affectionate American Eskimo dog, Buddy, is nuzzling me for attention, I'll sometimes feel very irritated rather than enthusiastic. However, for his sake and mine, I try to change my thinking and focus on his value. At that point I begin to feel loving and more appreciative of his affection. I focus on why he is of value to me, and at that point we both start feeling better.

Our thanks or gratitude as a form of appreciation acts like a psychological vitamin that enables us to take in the good things in life. If you have doubts about the power of what I call a vitamin, just take a week of your life and, as soon as you wake up in the morning, discipline yourself to make a list of all the things that you have to be grateful for. You will find that in the next hour after you have done this, it really feels like a good day.

It is obvious and normal to feel irritated if you haven't had a good night's sleep or discouraged if your bank account is in the red that day. It is also normal and healthy to deal with these problems by attempting to get enough sleep the next night; to take a nap; or to work on your budget so you aren't wasting money. However, the amount of time spent dwelling on anxiety can ruin your day. Negative thinking can also cloud your logic, sap your energy, and create a road block all of which keep you from solving a problem such as a struggling bank account by making changes that can rescue your financial situation or solve any other problem in your life. Gratitude or thankfulness can often replace dysfunctional worry. When we have appreciated what is going well, we have the energy to fix what is going wrong.

Stephanie, was a deeply despondent client a number of years ago. Stephanie frequently had suicidal thoughts and had made a few failed attempts to kill herself. She came from one of the most pathological families that I have ever seen. Her father had been a violent drunk who beat and sexually abused his wife and all his female children, including my client. His connections with the local police and other members of her family who were in denial enabled him to get away with this pathological behavior for years. Her family was NOT a source of love or emotional support. The family members in denial told her that she had exaggerated or in some cases had made up the sexual and physical abuse from her father. They almost convinced her that she was psychotic and a liar. However, her sensible emotional rejection of this dysfunction, adamantly denied by the other members of her family, left her feeling lonely, convinced that she was the one who was emotionally disturbed. However, she did have two close friends and she was thankful for them. These friends assured her that she was neither psychotic nor a liar and validated her recognition of the violence she had witnessed and experienced.

The lengthy psychotherapeutic process, which lasted a number of years, involved pointing out her courage in facing her problems, her intelligence, her good parenting techniques with her daughter, and finally her strength in being able to break away from the family pathology with no help from anyone in the family. After accepting all this about herself, Stephanie focused on appreciating her close friends. These friends introduced her to new friends and she was able to build her own new family of choice. She did deal with the pain of being severely injured by her father and by other members of her family who supported her father's pathology by denying it. She learned to appreciate the love coming from her friends. It was largely through the appreciation of this love that she came out of her trauma a much healthier woman.

Stephanie's story did not end there. She divorced her husband, who had also been abusive. Then, with her newfound self-confidence, went on to pursue and win a very large civil suit against a psychiatrist who had also taken advantage of her sexually. She spent the money that she got through the case on a new house for herself and her daughter and paid for her daughter's college education as well. Finally, with the help of more therapy, started building a healthy relationship with a an emotionally mature man who loved her.

Appreciating the Assets of Others and Ourselves

Appreciating your own and other people's assets is likewise important. An asset can be anything that you notice that is appealing to you; the sound of their voice, their athletic physique or, some essential part of a person's character, for example. This process makes it possible to build close relationships and create a loving atmosphere. This is particularly true when we mention to others, our appreciation of their assets. However, it is very important that we are sincere in our acknowledging their attributes. Phony praise does not build better relationships.

Our family tradition was giving thanks at the dinner table on Sunday. This was especially true during holidays such as Thanksgiving. My friend, Fred, will say a prayer of gratitude when we get together for lunch. It's a great habit. I admired Fred's habit and have adopted the practice myself.

We have control over our outlook on life by choosing to look consciously at what might be right, beautiful, or beneficial in a person, thing, or event. Unfortunately, it is easy to forget to refashion our thinking into one of a grateful attitude. Instead of taking a moment to appreciate the food that we eat, we tend to gulp it so that we can get going on our missions for the day. I'm working on this. It's worth taking the time to appreciate what we eat and, even further, the beauty around us.

The act of being truly appreciative or grateful drastically changes our psychological world. I am using the word *act* because we often have to act intentionally to change our thinking into a mode that's more appreciative. We often have to actively choose to be grateful.

If I am truly appreciative of my own talents and am humble enough to appreciate the talents of others, my connection with my fellow humans becomes a beautiful thing. If I appreciate my vocal talents and see these talents in others, it is easier to connect with pleasure rather than compete. While it is certainly true that there is pleasure in competition, being always competitive in all aspects of life can keep us from learning and enjoying other people's talents that are different.

I may meet a stranger who may not be as educated or as financially well off as myself. However, he may be brighter than I, have similar values, and have things to teach me that I might not otherwise learn. If I focus on our differences to the exclusion of the other person's strengths, the potential connection between us is tarnished, and, instead, I feel inferior or superior to this new acquaintance. I may lose the opportunity to make a new friend. With an overemphasis on competition or comparison comes the struggle for power, and this can kill a potential relationship.

Responsible Hedonism

I define *responsible hedonism* as seeking pleasure in ways that create physical and emotional health for me and those around me. This is pleasure that brings pleasure to others as well. If I get drunk and have a wild and crazy time but end up with a hangover and having insulted others, this is not responsible pleasure. Even if I don't have a hangover and have insulted no one, I still have put a toxin in my system which has undoubtedly been at least somewhat harmful to my brain and liver. Were I personally not a sober alcoholic, I might have a drink or two, and enjoy myself and others in a relaxed manner. This could be a good experience for my companions and me. In contrast, if I have a good workout then enjoy the relaxation afterward, I get the benefit of both the workout and the rest. The balance of rest and the work out enables me to be pleasant to others. This is not to say that all this comes easily. Hard work may, at times, need to precede healthy pleasures.

Barry, my AA sponsor, has validated elements of my quest to be a responsible hedonist. He has frequently shared in my pleasure over the things I enjoy in life. He is a bubbly, enthusiastic man who enjoys life and enjoys seeing other people enjoy it. In years past, as an active alcoholic, I didn't fully appreciate many pleasures, and this made my life much more mundane. I had every material thing that I wanted but my attitude was one of complacency and negativity. I rarely took time to appreciate what I had. Partly because of this, I was a restless soul always looking for more and not appreciating what I already had. This clearly did not need to be the case. I grew up with very affectionate parents who encouraged my achievements and enriched my early life with a love of music. My father, who was an excellent tenor in the choir and played both the piano and the violin, recognized that I had a love of music and saw that I had piano lessons. He worked with me on my shyness with people whom I didn't know by hiring me to work in his pharmacy. More than that, he would always shut down the store during my football games to root for me from the bleachers. Later in life, I often failed to appreciate my parents. Part of my alcoholic thinking was to always focus on what I didn't have and become despondent. Had I consciously focused on what my family had done for me, the good and happy times, that would have been a life-changing process for all of us.

When I started a new job working as a psychologist for a private special education organization in New Hampshire, I knew that the staff worked a lot of overtime. This position was very attractive with a bright, creative group of people and where the seduction to work long hours to please these impressive people was very strong. I told my prospective boss that as a newly married man I needed to leave on time at night to devote time to my new marriage. Of course, I feared that they would not keep someone on staff who wasn't enthusiastic about working overtime. To my relief, however, the director of the consortium said that he liked that I kept my priorities in order. I enjoyed working at that job for seven years.

There have been times in my life when I had much more,

materially, than I do now. Every two years, my wife and I used to buy two new cars. We would take the family on trips to Arizona, Florida, Bermuda, and other vacation spots. We had someone else clean our 14-room house. However, I can honestly say that, after getting sober for a few years, I enjoyed my pretty little one-bedroom apartment much more, and I achieved more peace than at any other time in my life. I have learned and am still learning to appreciate the surroundings that I have. When I take time to appreciate my surroundings, I feel the joy that I need to deal with the day with enthusiasm

I am not preaching self-denial nor suggesting that material success is not worth achieving. My friend Joe, who became a millionaire at the age of 55, has always been very appreciative and generous with what he had. He would be the first to tell you that it is his attitude of appreciation and gratitude that makes him happy.

Not Being Grounded in the Present Can Be the Enemy of Appreciation

One of the biggest enemies to appreciating life's beauties is the fear of the future and regrets from the past. To truly be appreciative, our primary focus must be clearly in the present. Obviously, we need to do some planning for the future and learn from our past mistakes, but the *primary* focus needs to be on what we are doing right now.

When I had a psychological evaluation in college (many years ago now), the psychologist told me that I had the habit of either skipping to the future or flashing back to the past. This habitual way of thinking, which involved worrying that I had stupidly chosen the wrong career and feeling extremely apprehensive that I'd do it again and end up with no direction. He was right. At that time I wasn't at all appreciative of my friends, family, or anything that I had already accomplished. While I've gotten better at this, 57 years later I'm still working at staying in the present. We can do this by trying to be totally being involved in what we are doing. When we do this and focus on the now, we become fully aware of the details of the present and are better able to steer ourselves in the direction of what is currently of value.

The value of each present minute needs to be carefully taken in. In our society in the United States today, we tend to move so fast in our attempt to get more and more done, that it is easy to fail to understand important details of what is being presented to our senses. Each moment is one that will never happen again with the same details and intensity.

A good example of this is face-to-face communication between two people. So much is said with the tone of voice, body language, facial expressions, and the energy of the person delivering the message and finally the words used. Without a visual cue the words could be easily misunderstood or taken out of context. This certainly happens all to frequently with e-mails, where the words stand alone—which has led to the development of emojis to add some context. Think about the statement, "Nice job!" said with an approving smile, That would be a real compliment. The same words delivered with a facial expression that includes rolled eyes and a certain kind of cynical smile, communicates disapproving sarcasm.

Taking the *time* to fully appreciate that moment will increase our effectiveness or at other times just bring us peace. When someone else is in pain and we can empathize with the pain rather than run from it, it is possible to also experience compassion between the person who's suffering and ourselves. The experience of shared pain can, indeed, lessen that pain. I believe this is one of the reasons that funerals and grief groups work. If we fully appreciate someone else's pain, we can be genuinely compassionate. We cannot do this without consciously rooting ourselves in the present.

There can be a moment of deep communication with someone we care about only if only we are totally present. This moment requires complete focus (much of it non-verbal) to truly communicate. The moment that I realized that my son had passed on (which didn't happen until some of the shock had passed); I also realized that his spirit was free and alive. I was then able to appreciate that our souls and all the souls that he loved would be connected forever. My appreciation of my son's spiritual connection eased my grief considerably. I didn't run from the fact that his body was no longer functioning.

We need to ask whether the pain we currently experience is necessary to develop better relationships, better health, or any improvement in our life or the lives of others. If it is, we will be on the right track to leading a less troubled and more rewarding life in the long run. The severe pain experienced by someone who donates a kidney to a friend in need (or even the minor pain of getting up at 3 am to feed your newborn) is quite different from that of accepting the pain caused by a physically or emotionally abusive partner. The first of these leads to a genuine improvement in the situation of others. Submitting to the latter is purposeless and destructive.

We need to recognize and face the pain which our mistakes can bring to ourselves and possibly others and try to correct them if possible. We need to accept our losses and the pain they cause us. At its most simple level, the pain that can come with purposeful exercise or working out to become more physically fit is analogous. We accept it in pursuit of a larger goal. The pain that is connected to these things is necessarily attached to them, and we need to accept that and move forward.

If we want to be well educated; physically fit; and a patient, loving person, we must be willing to do the work and that sometimes means that we suffer the pain that can come from great effort. When we focus on the pleasure of being educated and understanding things better or feeling physically fit, then we can deal with the effort or the pain involved as a matter of fact. The anticipation of the healthy pleasure is a motivator.

Mixed Emotions

When I was younger, I took a regular camping trip to Eighth Lake in the Adirondack Mountains of New York State. My mind would fill eagerly with thoughts of the crystal clear lake to swim in, the fire we'd relax in front of at night, and the catching of fish for dinner. However, I would also remember the soggy rain that could fall for several days, the bears that sometimes ate any food left out and scared us half to death, the unpleasant poison ivy, and a number of other surprises that nature also offered. Given all that, did I really *want* to go camping? Well, my emotions were definitely mixed.

If we remain fully appreciative of the present, we are inevitably aware of the cycle of pleasure and pain. This pleasure/pain cycle reminds me of an associated issue that comes up constantly in people's therapy – ambivalence or mixed emotions. I believe that we have these emotions about most of life's decisions. Do I want to go to work? Yes and no. Sometimes I don't, mostly I do. Do I enjoy being a parent? Mostly I do; but I wouldn't be truthful if I didn't admit that sometimes I don't. Many people have a hard time dealing with ambivalence, feeling that they shouldn't have mixed feelings. However, I can't think of any event that doesn't have some pain and some pleasure as part of it. The fear and psychological pain I suffered when I had to be unrelievedly honest when I first got sober many years ago stays with me still. I can also recall the two horrible weeks of six-hour days of football practice in the hot last days of summer when I was in high school. However, the pain of unrelenting honesty has brought me countless hours and many years of serenity and mental clarity following my first painful day of sobriety. I can also remember my pride in getting a full football scholarship to Lycoming college in Pennsylvania (even though I ended up at American University). In both these instances the joy in contemplating these good outcomes was stronger than the dread of the necessary struggle to get there. We can clearly benefit from the pleasure that is associated with making uncomfortable choices when the pain passes. We need to look for the pleasure when the going is tough. It is my firm conviction that most of life is far more pleasurable if we make responsible choices that may initially involve pain.

Recently, Abe, a client for whom—along with this wife, Julia, of course—I was serving as a marriage counselor, called me just to let me know that he and his wife were excited about the new state of their marriage. We had spent about nine months working together. For all three of us it was very hard work. They tried my patience more than once as they demonstrated no patience with each other. Staying on an even, non-judgmental keel throughout their ceaseless bickering took some doing on my part. The couple's constant fighting had gone on for decades, and their children had developed their own problems as a result. They originally started counseling because they worried that their marital problems would scar their children emotionally. Abe and his wife, Julia, were stuck in some deeply entrenched habits of communication, or should I say miscommunication. As they argued about money or sex in our sessions, just getting them to take turns and listen to each other was a struggle. Aggravating this was the fact that they were both natural-born leaders, making ceding even a moment of dominance a challenge. In time, Abe and Julia slowly came to realize that their leadership abilities could be best used in different spheres of their lives. Abe took the lead in investment matters, and Julia, who had done some extensive reading in child psychology, led the family in that domain. Furthermore, they learned to discuss each other's decisions with respect rather than dictate. It was a somewhat traditional division of labor, but it was successful for them. As someone once said, "Whatever magic works."

Abe and Julia learned some essentials of good communication: never screaming at or demeaning the other, always listening actively, calming down before discussing something controversial, and being responsible for their own behavior regardless of their partner's. Like so many other couples in therapy, they needed to learn not to interrupt each other and to stick to one complaint at a time when they were angry. Like others, they needed to learn to look at each other when they were talking, particularly when one was expressing something emotional and to remember that each one's needs and desires were always of equal importance to both of them. These new modes of communication were not easy to maintain, particularly at first. Although their children are now adults, the children had learned from their parents' experience and reinforced those lessons with counseling of their own.

Abe, Julia, and their children are now generally more secure, able to feel love when its given, and more creative. I appreciated their hard work and empathized with the pain associated with it. The pain of going to marriage counseling was worth the experience of a renewed and more loving marriage. Interestingly enough, about a year after they had concluded therapy, they decided to get a booster of a few more therapy sessions to reinforce their new communication patterns which required specificity of complaints, giving more positive than negative feedback, and never interrupting the other in a discussion. Old, less productive habits do tend to return, and they need our attention when they do.

Rejecting compliments

Unfortunately, when we do not appreciate ourselves, we don't trust the appreciation that others have to give us. Very often it is our misfortune to feel that we are being humble when in actuality, we are mentally beating on ourselves. We can then feel that we should be punished for our shortcomings. This mentality is often a part of a guilt-ridden life. We can easily see ourselves as martyrs and expect others to do so, too. We can at times even get jealous and angry at the perception that other people don't feel as guilty or bad about their shortcomings as we do. This boils down to something like "Shame on them for enjoying life so much, and being imperfect at the same time."

It is very common for people to consciously or unconsciously seek pain in one form or another because, through some strange logic, they feel that suffering makes them good because they are paying for their mistakes. Unfortunately, some formalized religions, due to the need for control by some power-hungry clergy, have taught that pain and guilt are necessary for people to feel forgiven and to become worthy of love and respect. Neurotic guilt makes us sacrifice at times when we shouldn't. A good example of this is the *requirement* of tithing (or donating 10% of your income for the support of a church or synagogue), when not tithing prevents a person from being a member of that congregation. I give to my church because I feel good about keeping its work going. However, if I were totally broke (as I have been in my life), I would not want to feel that giving 10% of my income was a necessary condition for worshipping in that church if I barely had money for food.

I do believe that very often we punish ourselves. This is one area where forgiveness and appreciation need to be intimately connected. It is often the case that we feel that we must meet a certain standard of achievement to respect ourselves and to be considered worthy of love. In reality, failure is often simply a step in the process of becoming successful, and there is no real reason to feel prolonged guilty pain for making this mistake. Experiencing some guilt that is fleeting to encourage change may be helpful. However, it isn't healthy to experience guilt that persists long after amends or corrections have been made.

If we can appreciate our own value, regardless of how imperfect we are, it is easier to forgive ourselves and those around us. Of course, this isn't always easy. Gloria and Art had had a number of sessions of counseling to improve their marriage, but we were making little progress. In the past Gloria had allowed her bipolar disorder get out of control by neglecting to take necessary medication to stabilize her mood. Furthermore, she had turned to alcohol to self-medicate. While at that point in the marriage counseling she had corrected both problems—efforts and results I thought she should be proud of, she felt overwhelmingly guilty for the way she had lived her life up to that point. She was punishing herself for her past and couldn't accept the positive efforts that Art made to demonstrate his love for her. Art had initiated the counseling, and, while he repeatedly showed his love, his loving affection couldn't get through to her. She simply couldn't acknowledge it. As we were at a standstill in marriage counseling, I had to refer her to another therapist for individual counseling to help her deal with her guilt.

In other instances, fortunately, positive reinforcement does work. I know this to be the case for myself and for many others whom I've met in Alcoholics Anonymous. Roger, a 23-year-old alcoholic client came to me with a very poor opinion of himself – something that predated his drinking. At the time we worked together, his parents were letting him stay with them because he had lost his job because he had been caught drinking at work. Although his parents loved him, they were critical of him in an attempt to fix his problem. After I had a conference with them (with Roger's approval), they started reinforcing him for each day that they tested his urine and found him sober. They also looked for anything about him that they could honestly reinforce for him. Roger had been a brilliant student before he had started drinking, and, with reinforcement from his parents and me, he started believing that he had a future.

He was in therapy for about a year during which time he stayed sober and went back to school now that he was sober enough to think straight. He also got a new part-time job. At that point, he didn't want to do anything to damage what he had accomplished. He started to go to Alcoholics Anonymous and to the best of my knowledge, he still goes once a week just to keep going in the right direction. He was able to forgive his parents for being hypercritical in the past, partly because he was able to forgive and appreciate himself.

When we see ourselves as worthy of healthy pleasures and if we learn from our mistakes, we may more easily accomplish our necessary tasks. In contrast, if we don't have some unconditional self-esteem which doesn't demand that we be perfect, the quality of our accomplishments will be diminished by a lack of drive due to feelings of inadequacy because we are not perfect. When there is little fear of not being good enough to be respected, we can be far more successful. Fear of failure often brings failure. When we feel good about ourselves without having perfect achievements, then winning or achieving a higher standard of performance is exhilarating, and we should, of course, enjoy it. However, when our performance is less than perfect, we should still be able to admire our own efforts and remain aware of our other accomplishments and positive person traits.. It is good to enjoy performing to a higher standard, but that is not necessarily a prerequisite for self-respect. We should go forward for the pleasure of succeeding, not to avoid failure. We must respect ourselves and others when our performance misses the mark.

Self-Deprecation as a Liability

One of the biggest barriers to self-appreciation is the fear, which many people have, that they will appear vain if they accept a compliment. I've found that for some reason it seems more sophisticated to sound a little negative about oneself. We should reject this cultural quirk.

How many times have you given a compliment on someone's looks or job performance and received a response like "you're just being kind" or "you must be blind?" Accepting a sincere compliment has ramifications for our mental health. Doing so, activates psychological units of fuel that help us continue to be productive. Saying "thank you" to a compliment sends a message to the complementor that they have done something good for another person. They feel appreciated for appreciating you. By the same token if the compliment is rejected, the person complimenting might also feel rejected.

Being pleased with our own strengths or traits of value is healthier if we don't make comparisons with others. "I am better than...." is *not* a phrase that necessarily leads to good mental health. As with all the four principles of mental health that I've already identified, Humility, Appreciation, Love and Forgiveness, looking out is as important as looking in. If I appreciate myself it is easier to appreciate others. Please remember that being humble means that seeing our selves as of *equal value* to others. This goes a long way toward keeping our connections with others healthy.

Nancy, a single mother of twin 13-year-old boys, came in for psychotherapy to deal with deep depression. She had just left an abusive husband and had to get custody of her children, get a job that would support her and the boys, and go back to nursing school part-time so that she'd have a career that would improve their meager living style. The members of her abusive family of origin wouldn't talk to her because she had divorced her abusive husband, and she felt singularly isolated.

Feeling like a complete failure because she had to go to Good Will to buy her boys' clothes and depressed because buying groceries for two growing teenage boys was expensive, Nancy's self-esteem was at a low ebb. Together, we worked to get her to focus on all that she had already achieved, and with encouragement in therapy she was ultimately able to admire herself and find other women in her life who reinforced her positive perception of all that she had already accomplished and done through strength and endurance.

John, one of my alcoholic clients who was an atheist, couldn't stand Alcoholics Anonymous because it placed so much emphasis on a higher power. Furthermore, he didn't like being in a group of any kind, an especially limiting factor, given that so many other alcohol treatment programs use a form of group therapy as their main tool for facilitating recovery. His anxiety over groups left him feeling helpless with his drinking addiction, and he hated himself for that and all his imperfections. In short, he felt worthless. Together we started exploring his strengths: He had had the courage to admit his alcoholism to his wife, to his family, and to himself. He had built a good home for his wife and six-year-old son and had supported her while she got her graduate degree in library science. That included taking care of their son while she was in school. He also never drank when he was alone with his son. Once he could take in all the positive things he had accomplished, his self-esteem improved. That made it easier for him to avoid escaping into one of his alcoholic "vacations' (as he called his bouts of drinking) and to appreciate himself just as he was. This in turn made giving up alcohol just another accomplishment that he could manage like all the others that he had already achieved.

Sometimes when I'm working with someone who is too self-critical, I will ask the client to imagine what kind of therapy she thinks she would have if my internal dialog said: "Paul, you're really not that good a therapist" or "I can't really help anyone." Obviously, my self-deprecation will severely damage my ability to help someone else who may have low self-esteem. Once again, using the principle of humility, I could not help anyone else develop good self-esteem if I did not appreciate my own abilities.

Gratitude as a Form of Appreciation

Being thankful is an important kind of appreciation. Appreciation in the form of gratitude is a catalyst that can help us fully absorb the good things that come our way. If you have any doubt about this, try saying "thank you" with conviction the next time something good comes your way. The moment we *sincerely* say "thank you," we can feel the joy much more deeply. As an experiment, try listing all the things that you are grateful for. You'll get better at it over time if you make a habit of it. I have found that this brightens the mood of my depressed clients and find in my own life that my mood becomes much brighter when I practice what I'm preaching here. In AA, one well known saying is "a grateful heart does not drink." Our whole attitude toward life improves the moment that we are grateful.

Making Appreciation Happen:

In a very real sense, we can train ourselves to appreciate the people and things around us. We can make an important decision to *find* the value in what we perceive. When I was very much younger, at the age of 20 I was hired to work at a residential treatment center for disturbed children. There, I was asked to work with Betty, a cranky, much older Scots nurse. She was excellent with the children but very critical and short-tempered with the other staff members. I decided to try to build a connection with her that was workable and would help me avoid always being on the outs with her. For about a year I inquired about her family and her past years in Scotland and sought her advice on things from time to time. I saw her kindness with the children, and I was impressed with her medical knowledge because the children in her care always surmounted whatever their medical challenges were. Seeing her positive traits in her care for the children and her smile when I asked about her younger years changed my perception of Betty from a cranky old lady to someone who could be very living and in some ways very beautiful. This business of looking for strengths and assets in people works in *any* relationship. This is true in building new relationships and helping old relationships to grow.

The only consistent way for appreciation to happen is that we must consciously take time in our heads to make this happen. It may be only for a few short seconds, but we need to stop rushing and take time to appreciate ourselves, others, and the world around us. As we get older this may be easier because we naturally slow down, but it's probably true that being driven when you're young often makes this more difficult. One of the causes for much of our unhappiness is the fact that our society seems to embrace a truly frenetic life. Appreciation of ourselves and others helps us bond with one another. Taking time to appreciate one another is well worth the time and effort.

When I counsel couples, as I've already mentioned, I very often have to start with the basics, encouraging them to give each other undivided attention. So often, in our desire to achieve status, higher education, or material wealth we don't notice each other's tone of voice: facial expressions, body language, or sometimes even the content of the verbal communication. Among others, I once had a couple, Matt and Alison, whose struggle for better communication began to improve the moment that they decided to look at each other when they talked. This became apparent when Matt was voicing some of his many complaints about his wife. As I watched Alison's face reflect her pain and the tears running down her face, Matt was too busy watching my face to notice hers. When I directed him to look at his wife and he saw her tears, he was grief-stricken. He began to cry himself and said, "I had no idea that you would be hurt by what I said or that my feelings made any difference to you." The more the two of them began to patiently listen to each other, without interrupting (which was big problem) and watching the other's face, the better their communication became and the closer they became. They began to be aware of *all* that their spouse was communicating both verbally and nonverbally.

Both of these clients were professionals who took pride in their achievements and had become notably achievement conscious. However, what they desired most was to be closer to each other. Their busy lives had been dominated by the pressure of tight schedules and multi-tasking while trying to communicate with each other. The magic gift that they began giving each other, which changed their relationship radically, was undivided attention and complete communication. Only then were they fully able to appreciate each other.

The Power of Really Listening

Wives (particularly those married to successful men) often say that their husbands just don't listen. It's been my experience that men do, typically, have a harder time listening than women because women tend to make relationships more important in their lives than men. Listening is a particular kind of appreciation that takes a receptive (and sometimes passive) mindset. Men, particularly ambitious men, have a hard time being receptive (or passive). When men do listen well, it's often only when some action is necessary, a job that needs to get done or a plan that needs strategizing. We men tend not to listen to the *emotional* messages that the women in our lives send. When a wife says, "He just doesn't listen," she is usually saying, "He doesn't appreciate me." This can then dissolve quickly into, "He doesn't love me." Many marriage partners, especially women, need empathy more than advice.

Look for the Positive.

If I were to work with clients and see only pathology (or their emotional problems) and shortcomings, I would not be able to build a therapeutic bond. If I first look for assets and strengths in someone, I have a better ability to build a strong, positive relationship between us. This business of looking for strengths and assets works in any relationship and is helpful in building new relationships and maintaining old ones.

This is equally true in parenting. Raising children is so much easier and effective, if parents constantly look for things to praise in their children's behavior or character. I want to stress, however, that compliments must be sincere. Dishonest praise can be harmful. Specific and sincere praise requires seeking out something what is good or right about a child. Children continue the desired behavior and/or strengthen their self-esteem because the praise becomes a reward. In addition, the bond between the child and parent grows. Of course, kids need logical consequences for their negative behavior, but this need not be punishment (which is physical or psychological pain). Very often just ignoring bad behavior is enough to stop the behavior if the infraction is minor. I once observed a special education teacher while she dealt with the distracting behavior of an emotionally disturbed child in her class. She told her class of emotionally handicapped students to "use their ignoring power" with the attention-seeking child. When the class dutifully ignored the distracting behavior the distracting one soon stopped his disruptive behavior. It was quite a revelation for me.

B. F. Skinner, the granddaddy of behavior modification, was able to condition a pigeon to type on a typewriter with only positive reinforcement. When the bird was merely near the typewriter, it received no reward. Eventually, the pigeon actually touched the typewriter keys, and with only positive reinforcement the pigeon took to its task of rudimentary typing. Punishment was not necessary. William Glaser, PhD, the author of *Reality Therapy* and *Schools Without Failure*, talks about building a bond with children and adolescents by giving recognition to their assets. These techniques certainly help in trying to educate children, as they definitely enjoy being around teachers who recognize not only their positive behavior but also who they are as people.

I had a professor who taught experimental psychology when I was in college. I enjoyed talking and being with him despite my finding experimental psychology a rather dry subject. He made experimental psychology come alive with his warmth and sense of humor. Quite simply, he made learning fun. Getting to know his students as individuals, he cared for them as much or more than the subject matter. Toward the end of the course he held seminars until 2 AM for those students who were interested. I succeeded in a course that I was dreading and enjoyed every minute because that professor took time to appreciate how difficult the coursework was for all and appreciated our efforts.

In my work with families with adolescents who act out or are considered delinquent, the parents often present a long list of behaviors which drive them nuts. Their acting-out kids are almost always starved for appreciation or at least attention. If parents don't notice or appreciate the assets, talents or strengths of their children, the negative behaviors become reinforced because at least the youngsters are recognized when they act out negatively. Although the need for positive feedback seems obvious, when it comes to our own children, we may be more critical than we realize. This is particularly true if we are critical of ourselves. If we are critical of ourselves, we can get critical of our kids without realizing it.

Enjoying our children is one of the most important things we can do in being a good parent. The quality of what we take in has a great deal to do with the quality of what we give or accomplish. When parents take time to fully appreciate their children, they get cognitive and spiritual energy to be good parents. Taking in the creativity, the energy, and sharing in our children's individuality and joy builds their self-esteem better than anything else.

For years, I used to run until I tore the tendon in my quadriceps and developed ruptured discs in my back. Now what I can do safely is walk. As I walk, I consciously take in the architecture, the plants, the trees, and the faces of the people nearby. I find this to be an expansive experience. My psychological world is a little bigger, which is always good. In a sense, I become at one with my surroundings, a very relaxing experience.

Being better connected with our inner lives and the world

around us turns us into artists of a sort who appreciate the beauty of the art around and within us and who can produce our own unique art. My life's art might be functioning as a therapist or just being a good friend to those around me. I appreciate life's beauty and enjoy producing some beauty of my own with the help of what my higher power has offered me in terms of health, love, understanding, and courage. I believe that our higher power has given us a great deal. I want to remember to fully savor what has been given me and use it to, hopefully, produce some things of beauty and value. I cannot produce good art if I can't appreciate it elsewhere.

In reading some of my early drafts of this book, my mother said "some of this book seems to be you working out your grief for Nick." I agreed. In adjusting to Nick's physical body not being I needed to appreciate what he was while he was here and what he gave me. He gave me affection, respect, encouragement, lots of humor, his own unique perspective on things, and appreciation for new music. When I focus on these things, I am grateful for the opportunity to have been his dad; I am enriched. While I need to and do feel the deep sadness at times, it would be a major tragedy not to be continually enriched by his gifts to me.

Appreciating the Big and the Small

In our attitude of appreciation, it is important to be aware of the big picture as well as the details of our lives. Appreciating the glory of the universe is as important as noticing the marvelous coloring of a lady bug or the wonder of an infant's small hand. We tend to be either abstract thinkers or detail-oriented people, and it is good to stretch in the direction that we don't often tend to go. The laboratory scientist studying microorganisms and the philosopher need to trade points of view to be truly appreciative of the universe within and around us.

CHAPTER V: LOVE

There are so many definitions of the word *love* that I feel it's critical to make clear what I mean by using this it. Love, in this book is an action word, at least in its strongest form. Love is an action or intention that helps us or someone else to be healthier, more fulfilled. I'm referring to the way love is used in the Ten Commandments: "Love thy neighbor as you love yourself." When a tired parent gets up in the middle of the night to feed a child, that is an intentional act of love. This is not always easy to do. It takes discipline.

So often in the office I hear the phrase "I don't love him (or her) anymore." Although I may not say it right away or in those exact words, my immediate thought is "start loving him (or her) now." I mean, of course, act in a loving way toward that person, whether you feel warm and fuzzy toward the person or not. Being responsible for our actions toward others often produces affection which may be more fleeting. Affection does not always follow loving acts. In addition, affection is not always a reliable producer of responsible love. When affection and loving acts work together, it is a beautiful thing.

If we love someone, we do things for the person who is loved. We hug them, we confront them if we feel they need it, or we may make love to them (if the mood is right for both people). Affection without action or intention is not always helpful. A loving action can be relatively passive such as active listening, but even that takes intent and energy.

We don't always have immediate control over our emotions, but we do have control over our thinking and consequent actions. Good feelings will eventually come out of good actions. The sequence that I am recommending is "think loving thoughts, do loving acts, and eventually affectionate feelings *may* come." I can't say with perfect confidence that affectionate feelings will come, but feelings of self-respect and self-love should be an outcome.

Based on my long practice with couples, it is my position that those who have lost "that loving feeling" will often regain it if they both think and act in a loving way. Unfortunately, in couples, each partner may wait for the other to think and act differently. I hear: "She doesn't think loving thoughts or do loving things, why should

I?" I also hear: "I can't act loving; I don't *feel* loving." My response is usually to *act* loving anyway.

We must be intent on thinking and doing things that will be healthy for others and ourselves. If I love myself, it will be easier to love someone else. If I work out for my health, it is work and sometimes painful, but it is a loving act for my own benefit. I feel better when I'm done but not always while I'm doing it. Once, when I was married, I went to the store for special food for my now ex-wife who was sick but who had made me angry. Overcoming the anger, I was doing a loving thing that may have only felt good when I had completed the act. The fact that I had done loving things for myself such as working out made it easier for me to be patient when I did something loving for my wife.

The biggest problem that I find in dealing with the concept of love is that most of us immediately let our feelings control our actions. If I don't feel affectionate, I do not act in a loving manner. I must hear the phrase, "I don't feel like doing that," a hundred times a day. In loving relationships, we must consult with our feelings. However, loving actions need to be controlled by our intellect. It is easier to do loving acts for someone when we are feeling affectionate toward them, but we cannot allow the presence or absence of affection to totally govern our loving thoughts and actions.

Loving Our Own Inner Spirit

The inner spirit needs to be cared for if we are to have anything to give others. If we want to have a good connection with our inner self, we need to initiate loving communication with it. We need to be able to do good things for ourselves. We need to be *humble* in seeing ourselves as of equal value to others so that we realize that we have the same needs for *appreciation, love, and forgiveness* as the others in our lives do.

Co-Dependence

One of the difficulties in loving others is that it is easy to "love" others in a harmful way. This type of "love" is co-dependence. Acting in a loving way is not always doing what a person wants us to do. Our loved one may ask us to do something that may be unhealthy for both of us. Sacrifice is sometimes necessary when giving to others but it should not go to the point that

147

essential things are sacrificed. When we begin to injure ourselves by giving, we end up hurting the other person anyway, at least indirectly because we don't want to be around that person. If we give too much, we can deprive ourselves of things we need and secondarily cheat others of being with us in a healthy relationship.

We can make a dependent loved one too dependent on us. It is my position that loving oneself must always be simultaneous with loving someone else. Loving may create temporary comfort for us, but if the supposedly loving act creates adverse effects to our overall well-being, then it is not healthy love. There are times when the ultimate loving sacrifice would be risking our own live if it means saving that of the beloved, however, this is an extreme exception that proves this rule. I would give my life to save that of my wife or child. In this case my spirit would be satisfied even if my body didn't continue. This extreme sacrifice is very different from working 80 hours a week so that my family can have a fancy house but in the process ruining my own health.

Melanie Beatty has written a number of books dealing with co-dependence. It is a very common problem. We are a nation of extremes and single-minded thinking. We also seem to have an unconscious love affair with the negative. You often hear phrases like: "give 'til it hurts.", "No pain, no gain" or "It is more blessed to give than to receive." Loving is sometimes painful, but often pleasurable. We cannot judge whether we love in a healthy manner or not based on the presence of pain or pleasure alone. Loving, although sometimes temporarily painful, eventually brings great pleasure. Caring for a sick loved one may be exhausting but if the caretaker is also being good to him or herself, this effort can bring pleasure. When the caretaker's need for rest and nurturance are met, there will be more for the caretaker to give with enthusiasm. The caretaker will also have a significant boost in self-esteem.

The Circle of Gratitude and Generosity

Receiving with gratitude is as important as giving with generosity. Doing loving things should benefit what is good for both the giver and receiver. If I am truly being loving, I am simultaneously making myself and someone else healthier. It is truly a gift to the giver to receive gratitude.

I have dealt with many people in the service industries and

healing professions (e.g., doctors, nurses, psychologists, teachers) who are often burnt out or exhausted because they do not take into account their own physical and emotional needs. As a psychotherapist, I work at keeping my own life in balance. I try to take vacations when I need to, take sick time when I need to, exercise, watch my nutrition, keep a healthy social life and spend time with my family. If I don't fill up on these things I need spiritually and physically, I have far less to give to others in the office. If I "*give* 'til it hurts" too much, it probably is not *good giving*. I may be making somebody too dependent on me and I may be on the brink of burning out. If I get burnt out, then I might start resenting the very person whom I am trying to help. If I thoroughly enjoy giving and have the energy to give enthusiastically, it is constructive and energizing to the recipient as well as to me. The loving energy is being sent out and comes right back.

Keeping love from becoming a co-dependency is the perfect example of humility being the underlying principle of mental health. If I am humble enough to realize that I need to replenish myself and accept the limits of my gifts, my giving may be far more effective. If

I view myself as the Grand Healer, I will run out of energy before the job is done and may end up feeling totally drained. In the process of being a good psychologist, I may need my own therapist to work out some issues that might be interfering with my effectiveness. I might need a vacation or more exercise. Loving myself by meeting these needs will help me be a better therapist.

Most of the people I work with show some signs of being co-dependent (not loving themselves enough). They are often feeling tired, crabby, depressed, anxious, because they are not meeting their own spiritual, emotional or physical needs. I feel it's important to remember that it is arrogant to feel that we are primarily responsible for someone else's happiness. We may be able to be a part of their happiness, and that is good, but to feel totally responsible for their happiness is bad.

Being a co-dependent parent is very common. Parents will sacrifice to give their children expensive toys, clothes, vacations and over time may resent the money and time that they have given them. As we love our children, we also need to love ourselves. Parents will often become critical and over protective because of the frustration, and anger that develops when they don't enjoy their marriage or friends, have hobbies, or get exercise among other things that replenish a person's psychic energy. In short, a loving parents must love themselves. Parents need to fill up on life to have something to give. So often parents ignore their health (mental or physical) and/or their marriages in order to give things to their children, and the children end up suffering right along with the loving parents. The airline cabin attendant giving the safety pitch before each flight will say, "if an oxygen mask drops down, put on your mask before helping someone else." The safety videos that have come to replace the live demonstration always show a parent with a child. I think this clearly demonstrates the healthy loving process.

The importance of "I" statements

The word I *is not a dirty word.* Unfortunately, in intimate conversation with those whom we love and especially with our spouses, we tend to avoid this word viewing it as a bad word that makes the user seem selfish. Actually, using *I* can improve communication. It also encourages us to love ourselves as we love others. There have been hundreds of couples that I have dealt with in the last four decades of marriage counseling where this has been a problem.

John and Merry and their unhappy marriage found my office about a year ago. Both felt hesitant to express their own personal interests. John liked hunting, target shooting, and fishing. Merry loved reading, sewing, and crafting. Each felt selfish wanting to spend their time doing what they really loved doing by themselves. In addition, their politics also differed—she was a Democrat and he a Republican. Neither wanted to fight, so they kept their differences to themselves. This led to both of them feeling trapped. When they allowed themselves to listen to their partner's desire to do something different, they stopped resenting each other and could more easily enjoy the activities they loved together such as dancing, good movies, and fine restaurants. They learned that they were not being selfish when they used the word *I*, and the tension between them diminished.

Communication tends to be much clearer when each member of the marriage (or, indeed, of any partnership) says things to their partner such as: "I would like to go on a cruise for our vacation this year. What would you like to do?" The *I* and the *you* are equal in a statement like this. Each person knows what the other is thinking and feeling. If they have differences, as John and Merry did, it is easier to make an intelligent compromise that meets both their needs. This tends to make for a sense of harmony with a minimum of unnecessary sacrifice. People who do not use *I* tend to be co-dependent and make unnecessary sacrifices. When there are unnecessary sacrifices over a period of time, the person who's sacrificing may want to leave the marriage because of feelings that they are always giving to their partner and getting nothing in return.

Evaluating Our Actions to See If They Are Loving or Not

Our society seems to have a difficult time blending emotion and intellect in a manner that makes for a healthy outcome. I believe that loving actions, which produce health in the giver and receiver, usually result in pleasant loving feelings. However, loving feelings are not always a sufficient guide to indicate efforts that are truly loving. We need to be guided by our emotions and our intellect to love.

I have noticed with myself when I have acted purely out of a feeling of affection, I sometimes end up giving in a way that is not very healthy. I happen to have a very cute American Eskimo dog, Buddy, who's a first-rate beggar. He has the routine down pat. Buddy is already overweight, but I have a hard time refusing him when he comes around looking for something extra to eat. Unfortunately for Buddy, I usually give in, which is not good for either Buddy or me. When my kids were younger, I had the same tendency. I also caved when they asked for money for video games which were far too expensive and in my judgement too violent for children.

Some of the biggest problems in having our loving relationships governed by affection alone pop up in dysfunctional marriages. I have been saddened many times by the fact that some very good, loving women (and at times men) have been caught in co-dependent destructive marriages, acting in unhealthy ways driven by affection. Martha, a married woman whom I worked with over many years, showed up for her sessions with new bruises far too often. Her husband was an alcoholic, and she bought him alcohol because she loved him and didn't want him to suffer the pains that come with detoxification. After his alcohol fix, he would be grateful and affectionate until a disagreement developed, and in an alcoholic rage he would slap her or at times beat her, apologizing profusely later after the rage had passed.

At times Martha would temporarily break out of this destructive co-dependent pattern, but after a few weeks she would buy him more beer, and the cycle repeated itself. I almost had to terminate her therapy because we had been working for some years and she was making no progress when she finally had the courage to leave her husband. She still loved him but finally realized that he was not willing to make the sacrifice necessary to get sober. To love herself – and to a certain degree love her husband better, she had to leave. Physical abuse, I'm afraid, can be as addictive as drugs or alcohol. Feeling sorry for the abuser and attempting to remove the immediate pain of the loved one is always destructive. We need to understand the logical consequences of our actions when we are act out of affection alone.

Another example of emotion governing loving relationships come out in families where anger and fear rule the home. These families appear very functional to the public but operate very differently at home. Rage is not always expressed as physical violence, it can also be through intimidation. Intimidation ("Wait 'til your father comes home!") can create an atmosphere of secrecy and emotional constriction and problems of intense anxiety and depression. Some parents still subscribe to the old adage "spare the rod and spoil the child." We love our children and want them to be well behaved, high functioning, and ethical. Unfortunately, if too much emotion is connected with punishment, it does come across as intimidation. It is far better to rationally help a child develop an independent conscience through logical consequences for their behavior (e.g., following the failure to eating a healthy meal by withholding dessert) and parent modeling. When this happens, the child can become ethical, high functioning and well behaved on their own without the parental intimidation.

Loving Means Pleasure and Pain

When my actions are initiated in a loving manner, there is both pain and pleasure involved. We have to be willing to deal with both and, in a sense, embrace both. If I fall in love and am ecstatic, I may experience some pain later. Due to my own human frailty and that of my loved one, I may hurt her and be hurt by her. I will make a mistake by acting unkindly, say the wrong thing, or on very rare occasions make a serious mistake that may hurt the one I care about so deeply. I will need to repair the damage in the relationship that may have resulted.

If someone I love leaves, dies or divorces me, I may endure intense pain. However, it is a human tragedy not to continue loving because I want to avoid all pain. In exchange for what feels safer, I remain in a chronic state of loneliness. If I am married or a parent and I work through painful communication problems, there is great pleasure in the end at being in a more secure bonded relationship with my loved one. When we have a physical break in our intimate relationships there will be a time of easier healing if we have patiently worked on our communication with those people. If I'm unable to resolve the communication hurdle and I have given it my all, there is at least pleasure in knowing that I loved to the best of my ability even though the relationship may need to end.

Many times in my practice I've heard a client say, "I don't want to become emotionally involved because I don't want to be hurt." If this statement becomes a mantra or a way of life, the speaker will certainly develop significant emotional problems. The head librarian for a big New England city, Sam, was deeply depressed and had developed an eating disorder, using food as a way to satisfy his need for nurturing. Rejected years earlier by a couple of women, at the time I saw him he wouldn't date anyone. His fear of intimacy had spread to the fear of being rejected by potential friends, even with other men. Sam had been neglected emotionally by his parents, who constantly ignored him. The only way he could ever function better psychologically was to start taking chances of being rejected again. Even with me, building the trust between patient and therapist that's necessary for a therapeutic relationship took many months. Just that process alone was difficult for both of us, but, of course, especially for him.

In another instance Jackie, the wife in a couple whom I counseled, had over the years become very mistrustful of not only her husband but everyone else to whom she should have been close . She had been hurt over the years but chose not to express it, and thus considerate people couldn't correct the situation by changing their behavior so that her hurt feelings could be healed. With person after person, she chose to cut herself off emotionally rather than risk further hurt. Her depression had become profound. At the time of our meetings, she had none of the support system that people need to make some therapeutic changes in their lives. This person might be a close friend, a relative, or anyone else we care about, but Jackie, with her fear of being hurt by those close to her, had no one left. I had to refer her to another therapist for individual therapy just to work on her beginning to trust people like her husband, who was truly honest and caring from what I was able to assess. Healthy emotional involvement can keep us healthy; the lack of this involvement is emotionally ill health. We are emotionally healthy as we are emotionally involved in at least one truly loving relationship.

If we find someone like Jackie who is never willing take the risk of involvement in a caring relationship with anyone, we have found a person who is always hurting and lonely. We need to choose the pains we bear because it is impossible to live without eventual pain. Acute pain might be involved in a caring relationship when communication breaks down but that pain may pass. However, the chronic pain which comes from never giving or receiving love may last a lifetime. Acute pain is involved when someone we love leaves or dies, but chronic pain is involved when we refuse to take the risk of loving and decide not to become emotionally involved.

Suicidal ideation can happen when we are not emotionally involved constructively with another person. This person might be a close friend, a relative, or anyone else we care about. Healthy emotional involvement can keep us healthy; the lack of this involvement is emotionally ill health. We are emotionally healthy as we are emotionally involved in at least one truly loving relationship.

I have a friend, whom I'll call Frank here, who is an attractive man who has met many attractive women who wanted to be his significant other. However, at a very young age Frank fell in love with the woman of his dreams. When she broke up with him, it was traumatic. Now he dates various attractive women, but he is afraid of taking the chance of being hurt again in the way he was twenty years ago. As a result, though he now finds living alone painful and he's endured that pain for two decades, he still cannot bring himself to take the chance of forming any real attachment to another woman.

If the person whom we try to love is physically or emotionally abusive and unwilling to change, emotional involvement is not a good thing. In this case we may need to move on to and establish emotional relationships with healthier people because we need it. I believe that if the person we have been trying to love is abusive to us in some way, then we can and must love them only at a distance.

If we find someone like Jackie or Frank who is never willing take the risk of involvement in a caring relationship with anyone, we have found a person who is always hurting and lonely. We need to choose the pains we bear because it is impossible to live without eventual pain. Acute pain might be involved in a caring relationship when communication breaks down but that pain may pass. However, the chronic pain which comes from never giving or receiving love may last a lifetime. Acute pain is involved when someone we love leaves or dies, but chronic pain is involved when we refuse to take the risk of loving and decide not to become emotionally involved.

(Don't) Talk to Strangers

We teach our children not to talk to strangers to protect them from potential harm. As adults, we still feel that potential danger (and at times, this is quite appropriate). Sometimes, using our adult judgment, it is a very good thing to talk to strangers. We can gain a good measure of happiness by fully appreciating the people around us and to think of someone who we don't know as a potential friend. Most of the world is lonely for friendly contact and making a decision (using our intellect to decide) to initiate contact with a stranger can make our days and the days of those we talk to more fulfilling. What I am suggesting is that if the environment seems relatively safe, such as a health club that you frequently attend or a church where you are a member, talk to strangers; initiate contact. This is one way to love others outside our immediate circle of acquaintances.

One day while at the local grocery store, I stood in a rather long checkout line with my 26-year-old daughter and initiated conversation with the woman in front of me. I had never seen her before, but I noticed that she had tons of groceries in her cart with assorted kid's cereals among the pile of food. I just said, "Looks like you're a busy mom." At that point she smiled and started talking in great detail about her children. Before I got to the cash register, this woman shared all kinds of things and asked me about my kids. I felt very connected to her, and both of us seemed to have had our moods brightened. As I walked out, my daughter asked, "Do you know that lady?" I told her no. She wanted to know why I would talk to a perfect stranger. I told her that it was fun. She just shook her head.

Calculated Risk Taking

I do not feel that we are acting loving to anyone when we're not careful. We do need to assess situations sensibly before we take the risk of being vulnerable. However, taking no risks at all to make new contacts is a terrible mistake. Appreciating the good qualities of strangers who may be potential friends—either passing or long-lasting—is important. Prudent and slow lifting of our defenses results in emotional intimacy and is extremely important to our happiness. We need to be aware that, when we don't take a risk, we risk not growing emotionally; we miss a golden opportunity to become happier.

Pleasure and Pain in Loving

Unfortunately, some people seem to follow an unwritten rule that, "if it feels good, it must be bad." This way of thinking tends to make us seekers, consciously or unconsciously, of pain. Living according to the principles I'm espousing in this book does eventually lead to a very pleasurable life; if not materially pleasurable, certainly in a spiritual sense. However, loving ourselves and others often involves both some pain and pleasure.

Two close friends of mine are successful therapists. The happy outcomes of their clients' therapy have brought them immense satisfaction; however, I fear that the pleasure they've enjoyed in their professional lives has led them to work too hard and too long. As a result of this over commitment to their work, I believe, they've developed both physical and mental health problems. They have become socially isolated from people outside their profession and developed heart conditions from neglecting blood pressure control and failing to allow themselves time for proper eating habits. When we feel successful in our work, it is very easy not to take needed recreational breaks. These breaks might allow us to function more effectively when we are back at our jobs.

The classic phrase, "All work and no play makes Jack a dull boy" hits the nail on the head, though rather than dull, we might substitute "exhausted."

In cases like those of my two friends, the pleasure needs to precede the hard work. This is a way to care for ourselves. If our intellect tells us that guilt is counterproductive when we have been working too much, we can thoroughly enjoy our time off. I can experience the pleasure of my vacations guilt free and later be more productive I have learned the hard way (after being driven to work ten to twelve hours a day for a long time) and not taking vacations when I needed to re-charge.

It is very often the case that there is some pain involved in reaching a pleasurable and healthy goal. Trying to decide what to do based on whether something is pleasurable or painful can be very confusing. The familiar phrase, "No pain, no gain," is sometimes applicable, but at others it is not. If there is pain in trying to change to make ourselves better at loving siblings, parents, children, spouses, or friends, that discomfort may be necessary providing that the overall end is a healthier relationship. In other situations, the pain is unnecessary and might even prove harmful. This can be true even in the context of exercise. I remember in high school football practice that we had to do an exercise called duck waddles. They ostensibly strengthened our leg muscles. Unfortunately, they can also damage the knees—and I have the knees to prove it. We need to logically decide why the pain is there. What is the pain telling us. Maybe the pain is a warning to stop what ever we're doing.

When I was first married to my second wife, I was quite possessive when she wanted to go out by herself with friends. She was very pretty and charming. I, on the other hand, was very insecure and anxious when she drew the attention of other men. My history with her made her faithfulness abundantly clear, but at that time I had had some deceitful women in my life. My apprehension about and possessiveness toward my wife got out of hand. Week after week, she would go out with friends and come home in a good mood and tell me in great detail about her evening. It eventually dawned on me that she was happier and more loving with me after these outings. I also realized that there were activities and interests that my friends and I needed to share that my wife had no interest in.

I recognized that I needed to venture out on my own. I had needed to sit with my irrational jealousy and insecurity and encourage her to go out. I could then be a better husband In this case the resultant pleasure was a wife who felt that she could be more herself with me. As a result, I had the pleasure of feeling closer to my wife. I was seeking the pleasure of a happier relationship, but I had to go through some discomfort to get to that state.

Focusing on a healthy pleasure to come in the future is a motivating thing to do. When we start a difficult task but are preoccupied with the pain that we must endure to finish the task, we will tend not to tackle it. However, if we look forward to the pleasure of having the task accomplished, the pain will quickly pass. If I feel that I must call my mother frequently because she is lonely, the obligation may feel like a burden. However, if I focus on how good we both feel when we talk, I want to call more often. Enjoying someone you love is a great gift to yourself and to the person you love. Anticipating the pleasure in loving myself and others improves the quality of the loving acts.

Love without Conditions

This is an ideal to strive for. It is important to remember that human perfection doesn't exist. I believe that we are healthiest when we can get into this frame of mind. However, when we commit to loving our child, spouse, or close friend unconditionally, we can love them even if they fail at a task or make a mistake. In this case, if we notice their imperfections, we are at peace. We can carry this out effectively only if we can do the same with ourselves.

Paul Ferrini has written a book *Love without Conditions* that describes this. I have read it twice and refer to it often. In it he focuses on self-love as being the center of all love and in many ways, I agree with him. At first glance, this idea seems radical. However, if we consider that the self includes a person's physical and mental health, it makes more sense. A loved self has a lot more to give to others. Ferranti's books have had a clear impact on my thinking and my work with others. This form of love requires the other three principles that I've enumerated above. It is possible to come closer to loving without conditions if we are humble, appreciative, and forgiving of the person we love.

Accepting mixed emotions is certainly an important part of

love without conditions, certainly a part of self-love. We can be intensely angry at the people we love. We need to love ourselves when we are feeling all mixed up inside. On the second anniversary of Nick's death, I felt angry, agitated, depressed, and at times sad. I couldn't experience my true sadness, partly because I couldn't accept my mixed emotions. My daughter, Gretchen, reminded me that I needed to accept my mixed emotions, then I could cry and treat myself compassionately again.

CHAPTER VI: FORGIVENESS

Forgiveness is a universal necessity that appears to be an important principle of all the major religions of the world. For Christians, it is the central theme of Good Friday; the day of his crucifixion Jesus is reported to have asked to the crowds of onlookers for God's forgiveness for the men who had persecuted and punished him because they did not know what they were doing. The message to the world for Christians was that they were to follow suit and forgive those who might do terrible things to them. Jesus's rising from the dead was to symbolize that his and the higher power's forgiving love had power over death itself.

Lack of forgiveness for people close to us who died, divorced, or in some ways separated from us can make the separation unbearable. It becomes a big problem. If we regret our deeds, feel guilty, or blame those who have separated or died, we have complicated grief, and that can control our lives. Forgiveness sets us free to live in the present. Guilt and resentment compel us to live in the past. One of the visual images that puts me at peace is to visualize all those whom I have ever loved as close while enjoying their company regardless of any mistaken hurts we might have caused to each other in the past. I often find that forgiving and acting in a loving manner toward those whom I have resented can be difficult but life altering.

Very often we hold ourselves or other people responsible for bad things happening when, in fact, there are circumstances beyond our (or their) control that were the primary cause of a bad outcome. When my son, Nick, died there was good evidence that he had a potassium deficiency. This is something that is apparently very difficult to detect in an autopsy. This very likely could have been a big contributing factor in his death. However, it would be easy to blame him, his friends or ourselves for his death that night because he was drinking heavily at a St. Patrick's Day party. It would be easy to blame: myself for exposing him to abusive drinking when he was younger, the people around him on the night of his death, his girlfriend for breaking up with him, or Nick himself for drinking too much on that night. Any or all of these things could be contributing factors to Nick's passing, but blaming does no good. Forgiving

Nick's intoxication, my own ignorance about his potassium deficiency, the mistakes I had made in parenting him, and his friends who drank with him the night of his death allows me to continue to be of sound mind. In this case, as in many others, forgiveness means letting go of our resentment and things that are out of our control so that we can focus energy on the present.

Forgiveness Is a Very Powerful Force in Healing Nations

Nelson Mandela was the president of South Africa from 1994 until 1999. He fought for many years before that to end Apartheid until he was imprisoned in 1963 as a political prisoner. As president he took a forgiving attitude toward the White minority in South Africa and devoted his presidency to reconciliation and equality for all races in the country. He advocated for people in his country to live in the present. This was not to say that he felt it was acceptable for the all-White government to have imprisoned him, but he was aware that, if he were to allow the Black majority to remain bitter about his imprisonment, the country would constantly be divided and warring.

Whether or not Mandela's emotions remained mixed and

angry is something only he himself could say, but his actions modeled forgiveness and reconciliation. One of the prime examples of this was his strong support of the Springbok's National Rugby team during the World Cup of 1995 when this team had been sponsored by the previous Apartheid government. The team won the Championship and Nelson Mandela presented the trophy to the captain of the team while he wore a Springbok shirt with the captain's game number on it as a show of reconciliation and unity.

Self-Forgiveness

I have come to the conclusion that when we have a difficult time forgiving somcone else, usually, we need to forgive ourselves as well. I believe that often when we angrily cut ourselves off from someone who has been a problem in our lives, **we** also made some mistakes in the relationship that we have not recognized or admitted. Once we admit our part in the situation, we can more easily forgive ourselves and the other person.

It is very common when we have intense anger or resentment toward someone else that some of this anger derives from our inability to admit our own mistakes and thus project all the blame onto the other person. This is called projection and is a very unhealthy but common defense mechanism. We clearly see the mistake of others but not our own which may well be either the same or similar to the other person's. There are other times when our self-blame is so intense that we don't see the power of other forces at work in a bad situation or, sometimes, the errors that others have made to compound the bad situation.

Many people whom I've worked with can forgive others but not themselves. I once counseled a man who had been an active alcoholic and lost his daughter after she fell out of a window because she was drunk and lost her balance. Because he had been an active alcoholic during her earlier years (he was sober at the time I first started seeing him), he couldn't forgive himself for not being a better father and felt that God had punished him for being neglectful. This went on for a couple of years. During this period, my client made a few attempts at suicide. When he finally began to forgive himself and realized that all parents make mistakes, he started recovering emotionally and was able to feel spiritually close to his departed daughter. His guilt had cut him off from both his spiritual connection with her and his own wellbeing. I suggested that he start saying: "I forgive you" to himself. Once he could do this in earnest, his depression began to lift, and he started enjoying his everyday life as a sober man, appreciating the work that he had done on his sobriety before his daughter's death. He began to realize that he had had a number of years that he had been a good and sober father.

Guilt (lack of self-forgiveness) and resentment (lack of forgiveness of others) keeps us from living in the present. I believe that the Buddhists probably do the best job of emphasizing the importance of living in the present. There are thousands of words written by many authors about the tremendous energy that can come from this. We get essential energy from healthy relationships and that energy is either greatly diminished or augmented depending on our ability to stop feeling guilty about things we have done in our past and resentful of the harm done to us by others. It's only when we are totally in the present that we can fully enjoy life. Without forgiveness this is nearly impossible.

Intimacy

I live and work in New Hampshire, which has, in my

estimation, its own version of the New England sub-culture. When I use the word *intimacy* people often assume I am talking about their sex life. Intimacy to me is a very close relationship where a person can bond with relatively complete safety. This may be with a spouse or with a peer of the same sex or with a child or with another relative. Intimacy is necessary, as far as I am concerned, for emotional health. This may be with one or two people in a someone's life, although having only one person as an intimate may be a sign that a person's world is too small.

Not being able to forgive is one of the worse barriers to intimacy. It is hard to be objective with some one very close to us, therefore in our human frailty, as has been said before, we always hurt the ones we love. When we love someone, particularly if there is a sexual relationship, it is often difficult to see our actions objectively. We will, out of this lack of objectivity, hurt those that we love, partly because they have allowed themselves to be vulnerable with us. We, therefore, need to forgive ourselves and others to have this intimacy flourish.

Harriet Lerner's *Dance of Intimacy*

I am very impressed and agree with the description of intimacy that Harriet Lerner gives in her book *Dance of Intimacy*. She writes, "For starters, intimacy means that we can be 'who we are' in a relationship, and allow the other person 'to do the same'. Being 'who we are' requires that we can talk openly about things that are important to us. That we take a clear position on where we stand on important emotional issues and we clarify the limits of what is acceptable and tolerable to us in a relationship. Allowing the other person to do the same means that we can stay emotionally connected to that other party who thinks, feels and believes differently without our needing to change, convince or fix the other." A forgiving attitude towards ourselves (which leads to less neurotic guilt) and others (which reduces resentment) helps to make this possible.

Guilt, Resentment, and Substance Abuse

Alcoholics Anonymous devotes a great deal of its guidance toward dealing with guilt and resentment because painful emotional cutoffs often lead to or maintain a life style of substance abuse. The alcoholic will use alcohol to temporarily reduce the pain of guilt and resentment, only to have it intensify when the effect of the alcohol wears off. The guilt and resentment increase with guilt over abusing alcohol, and more alcohol is needed to cope with the increased guilt. This is a vicious circle.

Once, I discussed a friend's alcoholism with him and why it was so difficult for him to stop drinking. He reminded me that alcohol was used as an anesthetic in times past for surgery. It very often would kill the pain when opiates would not. To stop drinking, he had to learn to tolerate pain. Alcohol abuse very often does the same for the pain of guilt and resentment for a short period of time. However, it also leads to the pain of emotional cutoffs from the ones we have loved, those we do love, and those whom we could love.

Forgiveness relieves the pain of loneliness in a longer lasting and healthier manner. When we can forgive ourselves and others, we have the all-encompassing relief of unconditional love. Feeling connected in this way is an authentic way of living. Paul Ferrini, in his book, *Love without Conditions*, does an excellent job of talking about how guilt and resentments get jumbled up together. He explains that we are all connected whether we realize it or not and then writes about the value of letting go of resentments and guilt. It is so hard to think of power being produced by letting go when we are so much in the habit of hanging on and attempting to control things as the right thing to do. Making things happen is important but not more important than loosening your grip on things that you need to relinquish. The serenity prayer is on the inside of my office door. It states, "God, grant me the serenity to accept the things I cannot change, the courage to change the things I can and the wisdom to know the difference." When we forgive, we let go of the painful past—our errors and those of others. Only then can we definitively enjoy the present. Letting go of guilt and resentments makes us strong

Other Compulsive Habits to Hide the Guilt

Very often the substance abuser takes on other compulsive habits when trying to stop using drugs and/or alcohol. Becoming a workaholic is very often the next substitute. At times, this is a mechanism of atonement for all the time wasted abusing substances. The recovering addict may seek to earn the right to be loveable by producing good things. There are ways that many people are addicts in the sense that they have compulsive habits or routines which keep them from being anxious and to block out guilt. One of the ways we can tell if a habit has become a compulsion is to deliberately stop a particular routine to see what kind of feelings may come to the surface. It is true that routine or healthy habits can make us more efficient. However, if the routine or the addiction keeps us from facing our guilty feelings and this is done subconsciously, the guilt will rise to the surface making us more anxious. Then there may be problems that need to be faced that stirred the guilt to begin with. Using routine to consciously control guilt or anxiety so that we can function is a good thing, but we must be aware of the causes for the guilt and anxiety and face the problems which we have used the routine to mask. Then we can function more efficiently by being completely focused on the present job at hand, whatever it may be. When we face our guilt, we need to be able to be forgiving first and only then move on. Unfortunately, without true self-forgiveness, we can't get closer to those around us and this makes us inefficient and unhappy.

Jesus was one of the greatest mental health counselors that ever lived because he encouraged people to forgive mistakes and live in the present. Many times, when clients are obsessing about their guilt but gaining some insight I will at times tease them. When they are busy saying how guilty they are, I often say jokingly ironically, "As long as you feel guilty, you know, it makes you a good person." Of course, I do have to take care that I say this to the right client because some people actually feel that this is a valid statement, which, of course, it is not.

Forgiveness May Take Time

When we actively chose to forgive, we need to let go of negativity and begin to be happy and more fully functioning. We may have to say the words: "I forgive you" in our heads and sometimes out loud until the feelings catch up. It is an ongoing choice to let go of harsh judgment of ourselves and others. The guilt and resentment will return from time to time in our heads and we will have to deal with it again. After a while, being forgiving becomes more of a habit and therefore a more natural way of being.

Some momentary guilt can be good if it motivates us to change what we need to change. It is the excess, ongoing, nagging guilt that continues after we have changed in a positive way to the best of our abilities that is toxic.

My good friend Barry and I have spent many an evening discussing our lives and giving each other support. I must emphasize, however, that Barry has done the lion's share of support for me through some of the pain in my life. One night, Barry said that "Sin is waste. If I am wasting then I am sinning." As the conversation went on, we both came to the conclusion that obsessing about our guilt is wasteful and therefore sinful. When someone is in the office for anxiety and/or depression, I usually will ask my client to put any guilt on a scale between 1 and 10. Many times, the number will be 8 or higher, and that makes it clear why they are in the office.

The primary reason for forgiving others is for our own mental health. When we are full of resentment because we can't forgive, we can have our vitality ripped away. We are powerless to change our present behavior if we are drained of our energies because we live in the negative past. When we forgive ourselves and others, we can engage fully in the now.

Addicts often remain active addicts because, while when they withdraw from their substance use they may be hung over or feeling the physical effects of the withdrawal, they also feel guilty. The addict often has diminished self-esteem. A person with diminished self- esteem usually has a difficult time changing behavior because doing so takes ego strength. To feel a little guilt, strong enough there's a motivation not to repeat the abuse is good. Unfortunately, very often the guilt is extreme, and the addict wants to give up and give in to more substance abuse to block the guilty feelings.

In the New Testament there is the statement that the "wages of Sin are Death." I understand this to be the death of the soul. Our soul is dead when we are constantly living with guilt. Forgiveness can "raise the soul from the dead". Forgiveness requires tremendous discipline over our thinking. This is the flip side of negative self-assessment being self-fulfilling. Initially, we have to realize that we have the habit of thinking that we are guilty and that often this message comes *only* from our own harsh judgement and no one else's. It's important that recognize, as I've noted above in several cases drawn from my own professional practice, that we can actively change our mode of thinking. We must be willing first to say the words, "I forgive you (or myself)" – maybe with the help of a mirror – until we begin to believe and to feel it. Then we have to act forgiving until we feel it. Being guilty is a habit of thinking, behaving, and feeling. Feelings of guilt only change when habits of thinking and behavior change first.

Guilt blocks love which is the essential food of the soul, the psyche, and our overall mental health. Humility and appreciation are necessary for love but forgiveness is absolutely necessary as well. However, self-forgiveness seems to be the toughest nut to crack. Possibly this is because we do not see ourselves in a humble manner. We sometimes feel so terrible about ourselves that we don't feel that we should be forgiven. It's sometimes hard to remember that we are of equal importance and value to those around us who are willing to forgive us. When we direct our focus toward narcissism (self-centeredness), then all we can see are the shortcomings of others. In reality, we're so self-critical that we don't take responsibility for our own errors because we can't bear to face them. We can then subconsciously deny our mistakes, projecting blame for any errors on someone else and the hard work of self-forgiveness isn't even considered necessary. Poor self-esteem becomes self-centeredness

One of the problems in understanding the concept of forgiveness is that it is often confused with excusing behavior. Harmful behavior or acting neglectful is always bad. If I have been dishonest, those that I have hurt might be more willing to forgive me if I stop the behavior. They also may not forgive me, but I have the responsibility to forgive myself, whether they do or not.

All of us can be neglectful or harmful; such behavior is universal. As much as we try, we will always be imperfect. Perfectionism (i.e., expecting perfection) is a mild form of insanity. Feeling constantly guilty is a form of perfectionism and therefore a form of insanity.

If our self-value is based on perfect performance, we will never feel good enough. We'll feel inadequate. Often when we are feeling bad about every little mistake, guilty about our poor performance, we will get depressed and discouraged and may become lethargic, or worse, non-functioning. The more we demand perfection of ourselves (demanding the impossible), the more imperfect we become.

186

CHAPTER VII: SPIRITUALITY

I am very much aware that there are many people struggling for better mental health who deserve to be happy but don't believe in spirituality. Some of these people lead very ethical and in some cases altruistic lives. I do believe that the first four of the five principals can still be used as structure for healthier living even when a person may not be able to make the jump to having spiritual beliefs. However, I have also found that many people who devote themselves to living by the four principles that I enumerated at the beginning of this book often develop spirituality later in life as a result of living by these principles. These principles stand on their own merit as reliable guideposts to happiness and fulfillment.

Michael Newton, Ph.D., has written a few books discussing a more scientific view of spirituality and even reincarnation. His discussion of these matters has been very enlightening for me. Dr. Newton is a licensed psychologist and hypnotherapist who has devoted many years of research to people under hypnosis who describe their experiences on the "other side" that the reader might find fascinating. My favorite is Dr. Newton's book, *Destiny of Souls*.

It is very interesting reading for someone whose views may be agnostic or atheistic.

If there is one emotion that I picture absent in the afterlife, it is fear. While occasional fear that heightens our senses can be instrumental in helping us stay safe in very dangerous situations, a fearful state is very destructive for any prolonged period. Prolonged fear keeps us from being productive and can create a self-fulfilling prophecy; the very thing that we are afraid of becomes a reality because we are so afraid that we don't take any action. For example, some people are afraid of having cancer; so terrified that they can let serious medical issues go undiagnosed, sometimes to fatal degree.

One of our basic fears is facing our more negative emotions. We may not want to face a rage that we have toward someone or deep sadness over someone we've loved. This fear is often there because we think that our dark emotions may, in some way, keep us from being respected or loved by others. Having a belief in an all-loving, all-forgiving higher power is very often helpful in easing those fears.

Taking Time to Digest Our Emotions

On the second anniversary of my son Nick's death, I was crabby and irritable. I needed to stop and just feel. It was difficult for me to do, even though I knew that I needed to. At some level I was fighting the emotions that I needed to feel by speeding-my-brains-out" (without any chemical aid) or getting-things-done. With some effort, I made myself pray and be quiet and talk to my higher power and the spirit of my son. I was able to cry and soon after that I was able to be spiritual once again, and I felt calm. I no longer had to fear that my grief would make me non-functioning.

A little fear is responsible concern; too much fear is crippling. Healthy spirituality that perceptually connects us to a spirit of universal love significantly diminishes this crippling fear. We all fear things that keep us from being at peace; financial failure, losing a loved one, failure in academics or love, are just a few examples. Belief in an all loving, forgiving, and eternal spirit puts things in perspective for me at least.

One of the biggest fears that we have is fear of disrespect. It is very common for people to risk death rather than be disrespected. Gang wars, even wars on a national level have been started over the anger (fear, turned into aggression) of being disrespected. Unfortunately, when we fear that others don't respect or will not respect us, we don't see that often it is *we* who do not respect ourselves and we may project this into a perception that others don't respect us.

Many years ago, during my first marriage, I had developed a close relationship with my father-in-law, who was both a psychologist and a Methodist Minister. Pop Farnell, as I called him, trained clinical pastoral counselors for the Philadelphia State Hospital. He validated and enriched my thinking about the relationship between spirituality and mental health. I miss the many hours of discussing the relationship between the two fields. Pop was quite tall, both physically and spiritually. He enjoyed life to the fullest and had a fantastic sense of humor. He and his colleagues worked at this state hospital for years and never seemed to lose their optimistic outlook on life in spite of the very emotionally disturbed people (many of them psychotic) whom they were dealt with continually. Pop Farrell believed that someone with a sound spiritual foundation would also be emotionally sound.

I truly believe that we are souls who are currently using a temporary body so that our souls can learn and grow spiritually. There are times when supportive family and friends are not enough to help us through life's struggles. Even with the aid of a psychotherapist, the support is not sufficient. We have many moments when there is no one there to listen to us or to give us feedback. In those moments we can feel very lost, overwhelmed with anxiety and dread. These are moments when, if we have a higher power to talk to, we can weather the storm. We may have experienced a number of times like this in our lives when, in spite of the fact that we have had a rather large support system of friends and family, we were unable to talk to them.

I have had a number of losses that have been life changing. Losing my 23-year-old son in 2008 was the most difficult loss for me. I have had to file bankruptcy and face foreclosure on my home of 22 years where two of my children were born. I have come very close to losing my brother and wife to serious health issues. I have lost both my parents, all my uncles, grandparents, and a number of close friends who have passed on. I have been through two divorces.

My friends and family have always been very supportive. However, in the middle of the night when there is no one around and I am feeling one of these painful losses, my higher power has given me strength and serenity. Because of my belief system, I am able to experience a moment of unconditional love. It is my belief that this form of spiritual psychotherapy is available to anyone at any time if they choose to believe. In spite of all the losses in our lives, we are winners because of our spiritual connection to others and our higher power. We all are, in my view, spiritually indestructible. Having a firm conviction about our indestructible spiritual lives is the ultimate goal for what I have called nice people to win.

In July of 2012, while on vacation at Hampton Beach, with my Brother Mark's help, I began to plan a memorial service for my mother, Betty Withington. The service was to be held that September 8 in Canandaigua, NY. The "Withington House," which was the name given to the parish house where my step-father had lived over twenty years ago in honor of all the years that he had served there as an Episcopal Priest. Bob (Reverend Robert Withington) had been a close friend of my father's when the two of them and my mother were growing up. My father, Al Wright, died when Bob Withington was going through the loss of his wife, Kathleen. Bob and my mother consoled each other, which was a natural thing to do for them because the four of them had been close in high school. They eventually married. There was always a feeling of deep connectedness between the two families much before Mom and Bob got married.

I found myself getting very sad when I started planning the details of the memorial service. At first, I wasn't even aware of why I had such a deep sadness. This sad mood was greater than when my father died in 1966. When I discussed what I was going through with my therapist, I realized that the Withington House represented so many losses that I had experienced since I had first visited the Withington home. Friends and family members that I knew began to flash in my memory. I had endured two divorces and had lost my youngest son, Nick; all three of my parent figures, and many other friends and family members who had passed on during the time that had gone by since I first visited this family house. I was overwhelmed with a sense of loss.

As I was doing my morning meditation in mid-July, my deep sense of loss was replaced by a feeling of fulfillment and feeling *connected*. I realized that I was still very much *spiritually connected* with all of those people that I loved because of my belief in the afterlife and the enduring nature of the human spirit. When I focused on that belief and could again clearly feel my spirit connecting with these loved people, my depression and sadness lifted. I was reminded of the practicality of this belief system in fulfilling our goal of mental health.

It is quite interesting that with 1929's stock market crash many formerly wealth investors committed suicide. Those people apparently believed that, along with their diminished wealth, their value as a person had been lost.

In contrast to this, it is at the same time obvious that many of the powerful leaders who have helped form our culture down through the centuries have been spiritual. The teachings of Jesus, Buddha, Gandhi, and Mohamed have been shaping our world for centuries. In addition, these spiritual leaders have, in many ways, been saying some of the same things for all this time. What their thinking has in common is the message that what is permanent is spiritual and giving spiritual matters priority brings peace of mind and emotional well-being.

In June of 2012, I heard an adolescent young man speak of his faith during commencement as he was joining the church. He said that he had learned that neither Mohamed nor Jesus wanted to be worshiped but rather seen as guides for the living, sent by God, as examples of how to live. I found myself feeling a little sad to realize that there are so many people in the world that don't have the same broad sense of spirituality as that mature 17-year-old high school student. One of the things that I enjoy about confirmation Sunday is that new youth take over the sermon time of our church to talk about what they believe in. It is so refreshing to hear diverse ideas about people's beliefs. It's a real education for those of us who are older, who sometimes feel that we've heard it all.

Neal Donald Walsh in two of his books, *Conversations with God* and *Communion with God*, writes about God talking to us through nature, the visual arts, music, and sometimes through ordinary people. Whenever we experience peace, inner confidence, beauty and love, God is communicating with us. Walsh makes it clear that what is *not* God is judgment, guilt (at least crippling

guilt.), vengeance, or shame but especially not FEAR.

Paul Ferrini's *Love without Conditions* considers a universal

love and forgiveness that are the only true principals of eternal

health. In his book, *Journey of Souls*, Michael Newton talks about a

God that allows us not only to love, be loved, learn, and be taught

but also to do this for eternity through reincarnation. Although this

idea may seem very much like science fiction, I would encourage the

reader to get a copy of *Journey of Souls* to check out the decades of

Newton's research using hypnosis and regression to previous lives.

These writers both discuss a universal, eternal truth that can heal the

most depressed and anxious client who may travel into any

therapist's office seeking counseling.

I am convinced from what I have been able to read, that most

of the founding fathers of the major religions emphasized, humility,

appreciation, love and forgiveness as the framework for both our

spiritual and emotional health. I can easily picture Jesus, Mohamed,

Lao Tzu, and Siddhartha Gautama (founder of Buddhism) discussing

the world situation in complete harmony. It appears that the need for

power and "more order" crept into the organizing process of the

196

formal religions as the centuries rolled on and the original spirit and intent of these great spiritual leaders often became distorted. The followers of these great religions in their attempts to "purify" their faith often began to see themselves as unique and superior to the followers of other religions. The crusades, when thousands of Christians and Muslims killed each other were a glaring example of the masses having forgotten that the Gospel of Jesus was a sacred text of the Qur'an. Moses of the Jewish tradition and Jesus were actually both considered sacred figures to the early Islamic people.

It is hard to imagine a God who is all loving, all forgiving, all knowing excluding any individual, regardless of their religion, or lack of religion from His (or Her) love and forgiveness. If a conviction is illogical, I want no part of it. As a very imperfect human father of three children, I can't imagine it being acceptable to not forgive or not love any of my three children regardless of what their beliefs or mistakes might be.

When we are grounded in spirituality, we will feel loved and forgiven, even when we don't get our way. Our errors, our losses and the reasons for our pain in life will continually teach us valuable lessons that will bring more pleasure later on. We feel lost only when we don't learn from the pain that comes sometimes when things do not go according to our hopes. We feel lost when we don't stay in touch with the universal loving spirit that is open to everyone who chooses to believe. It is very easy to live spiritually when we focus on our main purpose in life: to love and be loved; to learn and to teach. If we are humble, we can: love, be loved, teach and learn. We can appreciate and feel grateful, and forgive as we are forgiven.

The idea of spirituality is a difficult one to deal with when writing for many people in our culture because of the conflicting religious ideas and distortions that often occur in all formalized religious institutions. Believing in a hell of eternal punishment and also preaching about an all forgiving God (which is, I believe, Jesus's message) is making people crazy. I can't tell you how many people are in my office because they don't feel either consciously or unconsciously forgiven by their God for the mistakes that they have made.

I do refer to my higher power as God. The God of my understanding is the god of all religious people and of atheists, agnostics, and those who don't even want to discuss the issue of spirituality. It is a God that believes in us even when we don't believe in Him or Her (whichever personification strikes the reader's fancy). It is the God of unconditional love and forgiveness. It is the God that allows us free will but is always there when we need guidance, strength and serenity.

I am a sober alcoholic. I have been sober for a number of years in spite of the fact that most of my losses mentioned above occurred since I began my sober journey. Without my relationship with my higher power, I would be drinking again and probably an emotional mess. If someone is an alcoholic, the impulse to drink when he or she hasn't drunk for decades, can attack at any moment; particularly when there is no one around and there is a significant loss to face. I have a wonderful, loyal sponsor who has never let me down, but he could not always be there (mainly because I didn't want to obligate him) when the urge might strike. I must say as a supportive friend; I couldn't have asked for more. He was at my condo within an hour after I called regarding Nick's death even though his wife had just gotten the news that she had cancer. However, after that, there were times when Barry couldn't support me and God gave me strength.

In my 77 years on this earth, I have had many years of psychotherapy. However, in spite of this and my extensive training as a psychologist, I still drank abusively at times. It has been the form of spirituality that I found in Alcoholics Anonymous that has helped me make large changes in my life style. In my view, God is the universal spirit of humility, appreciation, love and forgiveness.

Continuity of Spirituality

One of the major ways that spirituality helps us stay emotionally healthy is to give us a feeling of continuity. Everything is always changing from moment to moment. When we really examine this issue, there is nothing in the material world that doesn't change: we get older; our bodies stop functioning the way that they used to; people die; people get divorced; and seasons change to mention just a few instances of that. What is the same? The spirit or true essence of us continues.

One of my clients was handicapped with cerebral palsy and couldn't drive, so I would see him at his home. Every once in a while, he would say: "I hate change". I would laugh and remind him that life was change. Shortly after my laugh he would start to laugh and repeat "life is change." I would also remind him that the love that he had for his parents and his parents had for him was eternal and that he also believed in God and believed very strongly that God's love is eternal. This would calm his anxiety. He needed a sense of continuity, as we all do, in the face of constant change. The belief in our immortal spirit soothes our anxiety.

Albert Einstein believed in a higher power that is eternal energy. He did not have a "personal" God. He did have the concept of God that makes for a perspective of wholeness and appreciation of our self as part of the whole, our souls being part of the souls of others. In 1954 Einstein related in his *Theology*. "A human being is part of the whole, called by us, *universe*, a part limited in time and space. We experience ourselves, our thoughts and feelings as something separate from the rest; a kind of optical delusion of consciousness. This delusion is a kind of prison for us, restricting us to our personal desires and to affection for a few persons nearest to us. Our task must be to free ourselves from the prison by widening our circle of compassion to embrace all living creatures and the whole of nature and all its beauty."

The Connection of Humility with Appreciation, Love, and Forgiveness

One of the things that I admire most about Einstein's thinking is that it is all inclusive and points to the ultimate conclusion of true humility, the realization that we are all in the same boat. If we're feeling lonely, it may be because we're not aware of this fact. St. Augustine said, "should you ask what the first thing in religion is; I should say that the first, second and third thing therein is humility." The Qur'an also conveys the idea of humility. If we are spiritual, we arc humble, loving, appreciative, and forgiving of ourselves and others. What is added to become truly spiritual is a sense of eternity and seeing ourselves as a part of that eternity. To me it is our humble, appreciative, loving and forgiving connection with eternity that makes us spiritual.

God

I call my Higher Power "God". Many people don't have the same name for their Higher Power and many others have no concept of Higher Power that they can relate to. For me, it is faith in our eternal connection with God that gives me a peace that is unshakable.

We need to be responsible for what we think and what we do. We have little or no control over much of what happens in our life separate from our thoughts and our behavior. However, we can have a very good life if we control what we think and do in handling the events that come our way **and** trust in God that the "bad" things in life won't destroy us but will, in fact, be opportunities for advanced learning. I believe that there is a wise part of all of us that is God within us and that wise part will help us make wise decisions. I believe these things because they work in such a manner that our lives become much better when we do believe in this God within us. We can see other people believing in these concepts and their lives become dynamic forces.

The Shack

William P. Young's book, *The Shack*, has some interesting ideas on the concept of God that mirror my own. Young's book is a novel, but it illustrates what I consider some basic truths.

In the conversation that God has with the hero of the story,

God says (and I am paraphrasing here): I have three things that I have some bad feelings about: economics, politics and religion. These things can draw people away from me. The problem that is addressed throughout Young's book is the narrow thinking of most formalized religions regarding who is good, who is bad, and who and what is forgiven. The book addresses cleverly the idea of our narrow thinking about who or what God is. God represents himself as an overweight black woman whose name is Papa to help do away with the narrow concept of God being an old man with a beard. In the book, God is a spirit of love and forgiveness that has qualities of both sexes and the best in human qualities. Another similar view I have with the author is that I believe that God doesn't control our decisions or the bad things that happen to us.

The hero's young daughter had been murdered. In the beginning of the book he is angry at God for allowing this to happen. I do believe that God gives us the serenity, strength, and wisdom that we need when we need to deal with things out of our control. We have then the ability not only to survive the bad things that happen in our lives but to use those events to learn valuable lessons that can help ourselves and others. I believe that the relationship that we have with this higher power can enable us to turn tragedy into something beautiful. It is the partnership of the will of our Higher Power and our own that can make this happen.

Getting back to *The Shack*, with the help of Papa the hero is able, to forgive his daughter's murderer and to turn his life into a life of compassion and understanding. Prior to this tragedy, he had been a somewhat laconic, unemotional man. He had to learn to love himself and others unconditionally even if some of the others had hurt him.

Having presented some of the negative of many religious ideas, I also want to add emphatically, that religion can be helpful to us and inspire spirituality, but the tenants of the formalized religion need to be examined carefully. A good example of this is the logical contradiction of proposing eternal punishment in Hell and maintaining at the same time an all-forgiving God. I am merely stating the conviction that accepting contradictory beliefs in any religion can be harmful.

Paul Ferrini

I am very grateful to Paul Ferrini and his ideas about God because he has helped validate many of my own. There are other authors I have mentioned in writing this book, but his work stands out as most significant in its validation of the views discussed in this book. In Mr. Ferrini's Book, *Love without Conditions*, he focuses on the power of love and forgiveness as the core of spirituality in such a manner that it becomes obvious that anything that deviates from those two principles is somewhat antagonistic to mental and spiritual health. It is important to point out that to Mr. Ferrini, love and forgiveness need to start with self-love and self-forgiveness.

It is from a base of self-appreciation, self-love, and self-forgiveness that we have the ego strength and clarity to love others. Seeing others as equally deserving of our appreciation means that we must remain humble. I am proud of being a Congregationalist but I feel that people in other denominations or who are atheists are as just as loveable or forgivable as my co-religionists. Mr. Ferrini's *Reflections of the Christ Mind* maintains, "Each religion has attached to it a climate of fear and rigidity that can destroy the tree before its seeds can be carried forth on the wind. This is true in any tradition. If you belong to a tradition, you must find the seed, separate it from the husk, and see that it is planted in your lifetime." Later on he writes, "Love, not agreement, must be the bond that holds the community together." We need to be able to disagree and still love those who disagree with us.

I wonder how Jesus, Mohamed, or Gandhi, if they were to revisit this world in the flesh, would comment on the formalization of their own traditions. I'm quite certain, from everything I have read about Jesus, that he would speak out on any rules that exclude anyone from worshiping in a Christian Church.

My faith journey

When I left high school in Minoa, a very small town in upper New York State, I went to American University to study religion and philosophy with, as I mentioned earlier, the intention of becoming a Methodist minister. I enjoyed my studies found college exciting. I had a very strong faith in God and focused clearly on my future career as a Methodist minister. However, I struggled during my senior year as the part-time director of religious education at a large Methodist church in Washington, D.C. While I enjoyed working with the youth in the church, particularly the adolescents, as I noted above, I did not enjoy that congregation's politics. In fact, they disturbed me. I Felt conflicted about whether I belonged there or not, I started drinking heavily. The incident that I related above about the Black family who was escorted out of the church one Sunday was a turning point in my career. Within two days of this event, I had not only handed in my resignation but had decided to relinquish my scholarship that the church had offered me for seminary. I went back to college to find a new career.

Looking back on this decision now, I wish that I had handled things differently. I wish I had tried to fight the issue of discrimination first before I ran. I wish I had discussed my decision to leave the church with another clergyman first. However, with my budding alcoholism, my thinking was becoming very black and white. I also gave up the idea that churches have any benefit and, in many ways, I gave up on the whole idea of God. Slowly but surely, I became an atheist and a functioning alcoholic. I was not drinking during the day; I had no loss of employment, no D.W.I.s, but I was developing a dependence on alcohol nevertheless. My spirituality was being replaced by a dependence on alcohol. Alcohol had become my God, and I went to my bourbon on the rocks for my comfort.

For the next several years, I worked in the field of mental health and didn't drink in any way that would threaten my license to practice. However, I relied on drinking in the evening to escape from the problems of the day rather than praying the way I used to do before my disillusionment with religion.

One morning, many years later, my wife confronted me about having alcohol on my breath. I was honest with her and said, "Yes, I was drinking this morning, and I am an alcoholic." This was, I believe, a moment of divine intervention. I had been denying my abusive drinking for years. At this moment, I had been given the courage to admit my problem. This was the beginning of a new faith that I developed in Alcoholics Anonymous. After years of heavy drinking, I knew I'd need support to stop drinking both through my new sober friends and a developing concept of a Higher Power. This new concept of Higher Power took a different form from the narrow view of God I had in adolescence. I knew that I needed a Higher

Power that was beyond all concepts of that can be defined by any particular church. This Higher Power had to be a forgiving God that gave all people the spiritual gifts to lead a full life. I would be having moment to moment conversations with my higher power to keep me from drinking.

It worked, and I have not had a drink since that morning that my wife confronted me years ago. I do not believe that I would have been able to stop if it had not been for my budding faith; the habit (or the addiction) was too strong. My decision to stop was, as far as I am concerned, a moment of excellent connection between me and my higher power because before that the idea of not drinking at all seemed totally impossible. Actually, I had convinced myself, up to that moment, that stopping was impossible. I had had psychotherapy, group therapy, and marriage counseling. Nothing else was sufficient to help me face the denial of this sneaky addiction.

I have hesitated talking about my alcoholism for a variety of reasons. There is still a great deal of prejudice and fear about this disease. However, not to talk about it would be dishonest. It wouldn't explain the big shift in my spirituality and my zest for life, which has been phenomenal. My previous writing was much more about humanitarian ethics and its effects on mental health with very little mention of spirituality. In my efforts to get and remain sober through the loss of my son, Nick; my favorite dog, Buddy; my mother; huge financial losses; a second divorce, I have had to rely heavily on my higher power. In the words of my older son, Peter, I've had to "fall on my knees" at least in my head to ask for help. After decades of heavy drinking to dull the pain of personal losses and feelings of inadequacy, it is not easy, but possible, to change. With the help of my AA group on Tuesday night, my sponsor, Barry, who is a form of saint in his own right, and God working through my family and friends, I have found the strength to remain sober. I also have found a new way of living (when I remember to put my spirituality first) that is truly peaceful.

The Twelve Steps of AA and the H.A.L.F. Principles

Years of failure to stop drinking in spite of intellectual knowledge of alcoholism taught me that—beyond a shadow of a doubt—often spirituality is a requirement for my sobriety. I know there are people who stopped drinking who are atheists, but I have seen thousands of examples of people who could not have done what they did in life without their spiritual beliefs.

When I started to go to AA meetings, I found the twelve steps validating, regarding my beginning ideas about the four ethical principles that I found so important. Even though the establishment of these twelve principles far precedes my ideas, I was not aware of them before I started this book. They contain very wise gems of guidance for life and steps to a spiritual life. They are an excellent example of how ethical principles can lead to a life that is healthy spiritually and emotionally. They are also an example of how certain ethical principles can find common ground with *all* the major religions of the world. In reviewing the twelve steps of AA, we can substitute the word *alcohol* for any major problem that might be standing in the way of our happiness. I'll list the steps with my comments in parenthesis, and you can see what I'm talking about. We did all of the following:

1. Admitted that we were powerless over alcohol (or other major problem) – that our lives had become unmanageable.

2. Came to believe that a Power greater than our selves could

restore us to sanity.

3. Made a decision to turn our will and our lives over to the care of God as we understood him.

4. Made a searching and fearless moral inventory of ourselves.

5. Admitted to God, ourselves, and to another human being the exact nature of our wrongs.

6. Became entirely ready to have God remove all these defects of character.

7. Asked Him humbly to remove our shortcomings.

8. Made a list of all persons we had harmed and became willing to make amends to them all.

9. Made direct amends to such people whenever possible except when to do so would injure them or others.

10. Continued to take personal inventory and, when we were wrong, promptly admitted it.

11. Sought through prayer and meditation to improve our conscious contact with God *as we understood Him*, praying only for knowledge of His will for us and the power to carry

that out.

12. Having had a spiritual awakening as the result of these steps, we tried to carry this message to alcoholics (or others who are struggling), and to practice these principles in all our affairs.

By following these 12 principles, many people develop a strong spiritual faith and intimate relationship with God. It is often the case that alcoholics new to the program come to their first meeting not believing in God but begin to believe when they try to live according to these steps. I know that my going through the 12 steps clearly helped me feel closer to my higher power even though I already had a spiritual foundation from childhood. It is important to say that the 12 steps were written well before I was born in 1943. I did not know what they were when I first thought about the H.A.L.F. principles. When I realized and became familiar with the 12 steps, I could see the similarity in thinking. It is unfortunate but nevertheless true that it took years before I put a great deal of energy in to living according to either set of principles. However, I know that I am forgiven, and I will proceed with the grace of having been forgiven.

Humility, which is the fulcrum or balancing point of a healthy mind, was clearly missing in my life before my exposure to AA. I know that I will always struggle with leading a healthy life, but AA has helped me *not* to swing so much between arrogance and self-deprecation. This is the swing of an unbalanced or unhealthy emotional life. Humility, once again, says to us that we are just as good as, but no better than, anyone else in this world. For me it also strongly implies that I need others as much as they need me to live life to the fullest.

Although the H.A.L.F. principles that I've been talking about were the core focus of my therapeutic approach to my clients before my exposure to AA, I can clearly see how these 12 steps address a lot of the same thinking. Both the 12 steps and the H.A.L.F. principles help me to stay focused on a spiritual life by attempting to live with my family and with those with whom I have other relationships using them to guide my behavior. Our self-forgiveness is extremely important because we clearly fall short of perfection every day that we attempt to do this. Staying humble helps us remember that most of us are living our lives the best way that we know how, which will always be imperfect. Asking God for help in living by these principles brings us closer to a fulfilling life. I also believe that the same is true for anyone, whether they are alcoholic or not.

Self-actualization

Self- actualization is the development of our personalities in such a manner that the majority of our human potential is being used. Our ability to be productive in leading self-actualized lives is sometimes limited by what has been given to us by others. This includes education, affection, physical health, financial stability, a life style that allows some leisure hours, and many other things that I'm sure I'm forgetting. However, having faith in a higher power allows us to often overcome these obstacles to our productivity and general happiness.

The Twelve Steps and Modern Psychotherapy

One of the most effective treatment approaches for anxiety and depression in modern psychotherapy has been cognitive behavioral therapy. To keep it very simple, the approach is basically: change our thinking and perception of an issue, next change our behavior regarding an issue, and then, third, the emotions surrounding that issue begin to change. Just changing our feelings first regarding an issue tends to be difficult if not impossible. What the twelve steps emphasize and what the H.A.L.F.S. principles suggest is that same overall approach. Change your thinking, change your behavior, and a change in emotion will follow.

We can think about the 12 steps or the H.A.L.F. principles, but, if we don't actually change our behavior in accordance with these principles, the change in mental health is cut short. Sitting in a chair and thinking about concepts by itself doesn't make me a healthier person. The same is true about developing a spiritual life. Both sets of principles require action.

Living and taking action that is guided by these principles requires courage. We need to make leaps of faith knowing that sometimes these leaps of faith may mean some temporary pain and discipline. Just being honest is an excellent example. Who wants to tell the truth when they have done something wrong? However, taking the leap of faith to be honest and being willing to deal with the consequences usually improves our connection to others and opens us to the daring one, the possibility of a healthier relationship with someone else, at least a better relationship with oneself. *A sound spiritual life comes from a life of action guided by these principles. It is also my true that an emotionally healthy life will come from a healthy spiritual life.*

Life is Suffering

The Buddha has been often quoted as saying, "Life is suffering." However, from what I understand, he actually said "Life is *dukkha*." *Dukkha* has three meanings: (1) suffering in the traditional sense of physical or emotional pain, (2) impermanence or change, and (3) conditioned states. It is my understanding that "Life is change" is the meaning that clearly makes sense. We are often upset that our physical existence is full of change because we look for continuity and stability and become discouraged and fearful because we see our physical world changing. The continuity and stability that we seek in the physical world can be found in certain general ethical principles that remain the same and that lead hopefully to a connection with our spiritual reality which is grounded in these same ethical principles. Humility, appreciation, love, and forgiveness give this sense of firm structure that enables us to solve the difficult problems of life. This structure is unshakable and can often lead to a strong spiritual connection with our inner world and the world around us.

Identifying With the Material or the Spiritual World for Continuity

When I lost my son, my wife and I were devastated. I still miss Nick a great deal and probably will every day. However, I firmly believe that his spirit is very much alive and that I can relate to him now on a spiritual level. I also believe that I can communicate with many of the other loved ones who have passed on in my lifetime. I can, to some degree, understand ancestor worship that is a part of some religions. I don't worship my ancestors, but I do feel close to their spirit of love and the lessons they have to teach me.

In the last 10 years, much has been written by physicians about their patients' descriptions of consciousness after their heart stopped. They often report seeing things while they were clinically dead which would be hard to explain if their consciousness didn't continue beyond what is normally considered death. However, I believe in the afterlife because I am a pragmatist. I believe in things that work. The belief in a loving after life improves people's lives.

Often people whom I know want to know why I believe in God and the afterlife. I tell them because it works. I'm not interested in things that aren't functional. My mental health has improved with my increasing faith in God and the afterlife. I have also seen this in other people in the 50 some years that I have been in the field of mental health. When we can accept that this material world is temporary, ("Life is *Dukkha*") but that there is also a spiritual continuity, everything goes better. Our anxiety and depression are dissipated by the knowledge that this material life is only the beginning. I'm not suggesting that we'll have no fear of dying or that we'll never have doubts about God and the afterlife. I do have my moments of doubt. However, everything goes better when we *choose* to believe in these things. I know that we're in good company when we believe this. A large percentage of the world's population believer in a spiritual world.

Doctors in their treatment of their patients use the same pragmatic logic that I used when discussing spiritual matters. How often have you heard your family doctor say: "try.....and see if it works; if it works, we're on the right track." We're on the right track when we see how our day-to-day lives are connected to that spiritual world because our lives are much more fulfilling by far. If we are not too provincial in our religious ideas, we can look around our world and see all the spiritual work being done through many faith traditions other than our own as well as the one we are most comfortable with.

This is not to say that our material life on this plane is unimportant, because it is extremely important to live each day to its fullest. We can have a broad sense of being spiritually connected when we treasure each day, take each opportunity to help someone, or do some good of some kind. Our day-to-day lives can be stepping stones to feeling a deep spiritual connection, sometimes the moment we begin an unselfish act to help someone.

It is also the fact that in terms of our mental health, the idea of just disappearing after being on this material plane for 80 or 90 years can be rather upsetting to say the least. The fear of dying, while it can be a functional fear, can also dominate our lives. If we are too fearful of anything, it makes us inefficient in all that we do. Something is missing if we are not functioning well. Maybe what is missing is a belief in an afterlife.

Humility as a Guiding Principle and the Major Religions of the World

Without humility (seeing ourselves as of equal value to all those around us), appreciation, love, and forgiveness are unbalanced. The principle of humility as a foundation for spirituality is very much present in Christianity, Islam, Hinduism, Buddhism, and Judaism. Religion stops being spiritual when religious people forget the principle of humility. When Muslims or Christians feel they have a monopoly on God, they stop being spiritual. The majority of the world's population identifies with one religion or another. My research on the internet indicates that the breakdown is Christian – 2 billion, Islam – 1.3 billion, Hindu – 900 million, Buddhism – 360 million, Chinese traditional religions – 225 million, and Judaism – 14 million. Those in the world that consider themselves secular, atheists, agnostics and just non-religious comprise 850 million people.

Although humility is a common thread in all of these religions, extremist groups among any religion who claim piety tend to forget this. Most of the world seems to agree that to deny our spiritual nature is to deny the fact that the world of material things is so changeable that it cannot be relied on for security. Financial fortunes are sometimes found or lost in a day. Health or life itself, in its material form, can be lost in a day or a second. If we are truly humble, we realize this fact.

To be truly spiritual we must be humbly tolerant of and open minded to the spiritual beliefs that differ from our own. There is no way we can be truly spiritual if we have the conviction that our group has the only true religion or set of spiritual beliefs. When we do this, we are being exclusive. We're not making those who differ from us as important or as good as ourselves. AA talks about the God of our understanding. This concept makes sense to me. It is a spiritual necessity to be tolerant of other's beliefs. I am fully aware that my approach to mental health is based on a "God of my understanding".

Having a sound spiritual foundation is healing. For centuries around the world, spirituality has been the source of emotional well being way before the science of psychology began. There is a core of believers in all religions who are truly humble. These tend to be the people who are emotionally healthy.

There are extremists in all the religions of the world who have some destructive ideas. These destructive ideas can become formalized and sometimes cause wars. These believers have lost their humility. They lose their desire to bring diverse groups of people together and heal their depression and anxiety. When this happens, the need for power creeps into these formalized religious institutions and thinking. A person cannot be humble and still have the drive for competition and power as the only guiding principles for life.

The horrible deaths that were the product of the crusaders' battles between the Christians and the Islamic people; the torture and the murder of the Salem men and women at the witch trials in our own history, and the bloody conflict between the Protestants and the Catholics in Ireland are some examples of this. I believe that most thinking religious people would admit that it is very easy to be religious and not spiritual. It appears that the need for power and the desire for loving those around us is a common conflict that can take place in any religion or in any institution in our world. While the spirit of competition may be fun in games of leisure, it disturbs our peace of mind quickly if this spirit overtakes our lifestyle and becomes the most important principle for guidance in our lives.

Spirituality is cooperation. It is seeing the universe as a beautiful organic whole. There is power that is creative and dynamic in cooperating with others. If there is healthy cooperation, individuals as well as the group become more powerful. Differences cannot only be tolerated but appreciated and utilized for the good of the whole.

The drive for control and power can work against this spirit of cooperation. All one has to do is to watch national politics as the Democrats and the Republicans fight over issues and the public suffers as has happened in the numerous attempts to get better health care for the people of this country. The individual needs of the group are not being met. When the political parties are busy trying to win the competition over who is better rather than improve on each other's ideas, the individuals' basic needs of both parties are not being met.

What is spiritual is humble cooperation that considers the basic needs of the different individuals as well as the needs of the group. The Christian New Testament uses the analogy that cooperation of the various organs in the human body to illustrate the fact that we all are very different in our talents and personalities but can organically work together. We all have a different role to play in the harmonious working of the universe.

I am constantly amazed at the knowledge reflected in other people's skills and my ignorance of those skills. The dentist, the auto mechanic, the computer expert (they particularly), all have knowledge that I need. Without their expertise, I would be lost trying to resolve problems in that area of my life. In the case of the computer expert, I don't know if I would ever even be able to understand what they know. On the other hand, when I admitted my ignorance of tax matters to my accountant, he reminded me that he didn't have any idea of how I counsel people to help them with their emotional problems. He counsels me with my financial problems.

Spirituality as a cure for Anxiety and Depression

We are continually being faced with losses and helplessness due to changes in our lives. That is why the Serenity Prayer, although difficult to live by at times, is one of the most valuable and effective guides to living. There is power and serenity in just knowing what we can and cannot change, particularly if we can turn over what bothers us to our higher power, if that thing is truly out of our control. Without this balance we are often feeling anxious because there are important things out of our control and we may withdraw into anxiety and depression.

The frequent result of realizing that some things are out of our control is that we can become enraged, trying to control the uncontrollable. If we are truly honest with ourselves, we can afford to accept that *most* of what goes on outside us *is* out of our control. How we deal with what is out of our control *is* in our control. We can control our thinking, behave according to this thinking, and chose to believe in a God of love.

The need to control is not at all unhealthy as long as we realize that it is *ourselves* that need to be controlled. When it is difficult to control ourselves, spiritual strength can again be helpful. It takes a great deal of courage to look at the things in ourselves that need to be controlled or changed. It often takes real effort to bring about those changes. There are many times when I feel the strongest when (at least in my head) I'm on my knees in prayer.

Having the wisdom to know when and when not to change, when to be receptive and when to be very active is aided a great deal by a belief in a higher power. It is not often easy to decide to accept a particular situation. This certainly is true if we are considering changing or accepting something about ourselves. We should seek the God within us for wisdom when our simple logic leaves us lost.

VIII:The Circle of Giving and Receiving

It is very important to "be" first then "do." We are forever doing, doing, and doing more. We find ourselves getting exhausted, depressed, and anxious that we cannot do more. A good life is one in which peace and happiness are the norm. This peaceful life is also an efficient life. The healthy attitude and the mind set have to be first. If we start the day by being thankful or appreciative of what we have received, we have more energy for the day. If we gratefully receive the good around us first, we have something to give. I've already explained the his energy circle that I mentioned earlier, but the idea definitely deserves a full chapter devoted to it. We need to meditate or pray *first* and *then* get things done to have a full life. Life is a lot more efficient that way.

A Daily Exercise to Try

One of the things the reader can try on a daily basis is to begin every day with a meditation that involves closing your eyes in a quiet place and spending ten minutes picturing all the pleasant people and beautiful things in a field around you, the beauty of nature, your health, the home you live in, the people in your life treating you and being treated by you with humility, appreciation, love, and forgiveness. See if, after ten minutes of doing this, you don't feel more relaxed, happy, and energized. You need to do this on a regular basis for at least 10 minutes a day, every day for three weeks. By then this will become a habit. There are obviously differences in the nature scenes and people in our lives that we're close to, but the process of receiving what is good and being ready to give back generously remains the same.

Recently, a woman my age who knew and loved my son, Nick, gave me a pink rose. This rose was important because even though Nick was very much a man's man, he found pink roses especially delightful. I thanked her and brought the rose home and put it in a wide rimmed glass of water. Of course, the rose only lasted a couple of days in the glass but its image is deeply embedded in my memory. When I want to feel connected with Nick and the spirit of love in the universe, I focus on the vivid memory of that rose. I also try to remember this lady's kindness to me, and I am grateful.

One fall day this past year, I backed into a car in the parking lot of my office. Because it was obviously a bumper to bumper light contact, I started to pull out without much concern. However, I thought about it more because I had to stop for a red light anyway and decided to turn around and check for damage. While I was in the process of turning around to examine the bumped car, a lady in the parking lot started screaming: "There is damage to my car," pointing to the grey vehicle that I had just backed into. I rolled down my window and said: "Thank you for letting me know." I parked my car and began to assess the damage. The other person's car bumper was actually cracked, a cheap plastic bumper, I guess. Mine was okay. She was already in the process of calling the police. I told her I was surprised that there was any damage but assured her that I was appreciative of her pointing to the problem.

The next thing I knew, as we were waiting for the police, she started to talk about her recent divorce. She asked if I worked in the building and I told her that I worked as a psychologist on the second floor. She proceeded to talk about her life and she began to cry. She then asked for my business card and smiled saying that she would be calling for an appointment. I told her that I didn't think that I had anything open but if there was a time open, I would be happy to see her. We both agreed that we had enjoyed talking to each other.

This situation made an impact on me. What had started out as a tense situation, actually ended up in a nice, friendly, communication. I was thankful that I had not gotten defensive about her screaming and that she had explained that someone recently had hit her car when it had been parked and driven off. We both had made an attempt to be humble and considerate. It paid off.

At any rate, we both took the chance to humbly relate in a caring manner and it made our day. She received my care for her and I received her good will. I saw and received what is underneath her anger which was the fear of being taken advantage of and she showed her appreciation for this.

So often we are admired for being a giving and sacrificing person. As the importance of receiving with appreciation is often given less importance, it seems appropriate to stress to the reader that giving with generosity and receiving with gratitude are equally important, This circle can keep us healthy. Giving generously and receiving gratefully based on the principle of humility (I am of equal

value too all others and need to be treated so) is how being "nice"

makes us happy.

IX: Pulling It All Together

Life can seem so complicated, stressful, and downright overwhelming. One of the best pieces of advice mentioned often in AA is and has been "Keep it simple." If we have some simple guiding principles that we can *consistently* live by, we can do just that. Living by the principles of humility, appreciation, love, forgiveness and graduating to a spiritual life allows us to love and be loved, to learn, and to teach unfettered by crippling negative emotion that robs us of serenity and joy.

In Chapter Seven considering the importance of a spiritual life is, by no means, meant to detract from the reality of everyday problems and work. At times this can seem very mundane. Our spiritual life doesn't mean much if it simply becomes the "opiate of the masses" as religion has sometimes been described. It should be a state of mind of being lovingly connected to the world around us. We must be able to clean the cat box, help with the dishes, work on the taxes, and handle every other mundane chore that comes our way to be able to live a meaningful and enjoyable life. We need to keep our heads connected to our spiritual values and be led by them while we are doing the dishes. We need to creatively deal with the mundane jobs in our lives in such a manner that we add the spirit of love to these labors so that they take on a spiritual significance. Doing the dishes and cleaning the cat box take on a sense of accomplishment and joy if we can connect with the sense of order that we are helping establish for ourselves, our pets, and our family. Our spiritual frame of mind can guide all that we think, feel, and do. If we are to lead a fully rich and spiritual life, we just need to be fully aware of that connection.

The universe is good. We need to be consistently aware of its goodness. To do this, we can take a leap of faith and say "I believe." This is a conscious choice. If we say, "Life sucks and then you die," that belief will govern our mood. I maintain the former belief because I see strong evidence that belief in a good universe brings happiness, meaning, and health.

If readers are going to take away something helpful from this book, I want them to understand that being emotionally healthy is often easier to understand than to accomplish. People of less than average intellectual acuity and sometimes small children can often generally understand what it takes to be emotionally healthy, but often it takes discipline to follow through with the necessary actions.

Focusing on humility, appreciation, love and forgiveness often takes the support of others. This is true for the gifted intellectual and the intellectually challenged. Leading our lives by these four guiding principles often takes discipline and courage. This is particularly true when we focus on remaining humble and realizing that we must appreciate, love and forgive ourselves. Friends and family can help us with that. Loving our neighbors *as* we love ourselves is not easy but quite possible when we help each other.

When we listen to wisdom from people who are younger, older, less educated, or less well off than we are and *humbly appreciate* that wisdom, we are enjoying life and living it to the fullest in that moment. So often wisdom comes from what seems to be strange places. How often have children said profound things that we all need to hear but dismiss their voices because they are only children?

I have to forgive my own lack of humility when I think of all the years that I dismissed the idea that I needed help with my drinking addiction when I was busy giving advice to others about their problems. We must continue to learn humbly if we are to teach effectively. Some of the most important lessons that we are frequently taught and re-taught in life have come from people who were less fortunate and less educated than we are.

We need to become actively involved in this good universe. Refusing to be a litterbug is an example. If we are in a hurry to get things done, often we may not bother to pick up a receipt that dropped out of a bag of things that we had just purchased. When we try to be aware of how we affect others by our actions, we may realize that we are much happier if we take the time to pick up what we dropped. If we are walking down the street and see someone struggling with a bag of groceries while trying to open a door, we feel better taking the time to help out. We become a little happier when we try to respect the connection with our environment. By handling ourselves in these ways, we're living in a loving manner. These seemingly insignificant things add up, and our decisions about handling them in a spiritual manner will make us happy. When we don't pay attention to our effect on the world, it makes us feel that we're on a treadmill, doing the same repetitive tasks, day in and day out—a good way to become anxious and depressed.

Being aware and enjoying the connection with the universe makes us truly happy and healthy. We are connected with all that is within us and around us. Being fully aware of this connection enables us to maximize the quality of this connection, making life an exciting and happy journey.

We may have many painful and sometimes tragic things happen to us. These events can be used to our advantage if we keep the four principles at the center of our thinking at all times and let them lead us to a spiritual life. The physical death of my son has forced me to be aware of the necessity of this way of living. I certainly am no saint, and there have been times when I have not directed my thinking using these principles and disconnected myself from my spiritual life. This has always had the result of making me feel discouraged and grumpy and function less efficiently. As I said earlier, I am a pragmatist. I believe in doing what works. If we live this way, moment to moment, we are enjoying life. If we do not, we can easily become depressed, bored, and grumpy.

One of the main ideas that I am hoping to convey is that a meaningful life is one where the journey is spiritual; that is the goal. This is not to say that specific goals of education, financial security, and professional goals are unimportant. The journey itself, the interactions that we make along the way to these goals, are more important. The reasons for our goals, how we treat other people while reaching these goals, and our attitude while achieving these goals are all more important than the goals themselves. Physical life is a very terminal matter. Where we are at the moment in our connection with those around us moment to moment is what makes life full or empty. If I rush to get my son to school and experience no sense of bonding with him while accomplishing this task, I will have a moment of spiritual emptiness. If I relate to him in a loving manner on the way to school, I feel emotionally full.

People come to my office because they are anxious and/or depressed. This means that they are afraid of people or events and are feeling helpless. They long for the security of deep contact with those who are important to them. When they feel secure in the deep contact that they have with others, they are not as bothered by their fears of issues that are out of their control.

Between the Pleasure and the Pain of life

We need to accept the fact that we are never truly alone unless we chose to be. We are always capable of a beautiful contact with those around us. This keeps our lives full of joy. We can always have this joyful life if we put the basic four principles into play and let them guide our every action in dealing with our inner self and with those around us. This is how we can find our stability and peace.

Most pleasures will pass; most pain will also pass. However, the sense of a rich, loving connection can remain constant by diligently disciplining where we allow our minds to focus. It is very easy to allow pleasure or pain to separate us from our loving relationships. Clearly, drugs, alcohol, expensive toys, and engrossing hobbies (golf, internet games, etc.) can be very pleasurable and grab our attention completely. Relationships can be destroyed by being left unattended. The psychological pain of a deceased loved one, divorce, or loss of a career can be devastating to our focus on relationships. Physical pain can clearly do this. It is both during the acute peaks and valleys of the pleasure/pain continuum that we need most to remember to focus on the quality of our relationships.

The Illusion and the Reality of Permanency

One of the most common causes for the psychological pain that we suffer is being disillusioned by the illusion of permanency. As I discussed before, I believe that we all have some sense of a need for permanency. Unfortunately, almost everything is always changing. When we realize that someone we love very much has died: when we suddenly realize that we are going to die, when we lose a lifelong career, or when a 30-year marriage ends in divorce, our whole world is totally different, or so it seems initially. We tend to be in acute psychological pain accompanied by depression and/or anxiety. We live with the illusion that we will always have our children, our spouses, our family, and our friends in the current state of material solidarity. We are traumatized when we realize that this material solidarity has been only temporary.

The real permanency is spiritual or pure energy. According to Einstein and most of the scientific world, the sum of energy and mass, remains the same. Energy does not go away; it just changes form. God or the spirit of love does not go away but, in fact, changes form. Our deceased children, parents, grandparents, aunts, and uncles have merely changed form to pure energy.

We are all basically pure energy; we are connected, but to be at peace we must be willing to visualize and live in the reality of connection. We all have the power to do this if we are willing. It is my belief that, when we put spirituality as a last priority or exclude it all together by denying that a spiritual life is even possible, we can become anxious and depressed. Visualizing only the material world is living in an illusion. The material world is only one temporary form of energy. However, energy itself is eternal. However, even the most atheistic scientist will admit that there is far more energy in the world than that which can be perceived by the five senses.

Whether we are Christian, Buddhist, or atheist, we can be guided by the four principles of humility, appreciation, love, forgiveness and hopefully, this will often lead to a spiritual life. We can use these principles to guide our connection with ourselves and others. Our world will begin to correct itself. We can be humble enough to realize that the tragedy that has happened to us has always happened to others and pursue and receive the emotional support that we need. We can be grateful that there are people around us who love us. We can be glad about the good years that we had with those who have passed on. We can do loving acts for others and ourselves that keep us and them healthy. We can forgive ourselves and the people who have passed on for not making our relationships more meaningful. We may even have to forgive them for dying and for the things that they left undone. We also need to forgive ourselves for the things we did or didn't do for our deceased loved ones. These five principles don't change.

Being in the Present is the "Present"

Living according to the four principles requires us, to live in the present. We cannot be humbly appreciative, loving, and forgiving of ourselves and others if we are not consciously focusing on the present. How can I appreciate a beautiful sunset or a beautiful person if I am thinking about my job or the taxes that I owe?

The gift of living in the present puts us where we are most powerful and most fully alive. We are then in the only time zone where we can "have the courage of change the things that we can" that is mentioned in the Serenity Prayer. Letting go of the past and (to a large degree) the outcome of the future also becomes more possible. To have the "wisdom to know the difference" between what we can and can't change, we do need to make reference to the past and the future briefly to learn from the past and consider the probable consequences of our actions. However, an ethical life must be led primarily in the present to be effective. This helps us avoid being depressed about our past or anxious about our future. It is the only way to live effectively. The present is quickly becoming the past and moving into the future. It is quite the paradox that being aware and totally accepting the constant changing within and around us, that we can remain emotionally stable.

Our Internal Drill Sergeant

My father was a drill sergeant in the army during World War II. When he came back from Germany, he still had many of the tough attitudes that a combat sergeant would have. Some of this was incorporated into his style of parenting. When Dad gave an order, we obeyed without question. As an adolescent, this was quite uncomfortable at times, although, to his credit, he modified this attitude considerably as my brother and I got older. I have learned, however, to appreciate the discipline of the drill sergeant that I internalized as a youth. It seems to help me get through difficult times.

When we are depressed, we often don't want to do anything. We need to develop an internal drill sergeant for these times that will jump-start our daily activities. I'm talking about a tough internal voice that commands, "Move!" or "You have a life to live!" That voice isn't always necessary but when boredom or depression sets in, we need to jolt ourselves into action. The guiding principles can only keep our lives meaningful and rich if we are willing to do what we need to do and to relate to others even when we feel like withdrawing. There are times when crippling depression makes anti-depressant medication a healthy adjunct to energize this "drill sergeant," but there is no substitute for commanding ourselves internally. While the majority of this book is about giving and taking support through ethical relationships, we do have to command ourselves to do things that are hard to do.

I believe that it's important to add that we do not allow our internal drill sergeant to be overly critical or negative. Very self-critical messages are not helpful. However, tough, positive self-talk can be very instrumental in getting us going. I'm talking about positive statements like: "You can do this!" "Do it now!" or "I am the captain of my ship!"

The problem with changing in a positive direction is inertia or the strong tendency to continue to go in the same direction at the same speed or just to do nothing. We need to produce a strong internal force or *chi*, as Chinese philosophers would put it, to overcome this inertia and do something new. It is very important to realize that sometimes we need this disciplined drill sergeant to give the directive to slow down or stop a particular compulsive pattern of thinking or movement. We need to break the psychological and dysfunctional inertia that leads to remaining still or the compulsive movement in our activities.

A good deal of this inertia has anxiety attached to it because there is usually a fear of the unknown. Sometimes we can be like the deer in the headlights of an oncoming car. Inertia also tends to be comfortable. If we have always exercised daily, then we want to continue that. If we have always watched TV, we tend to do that. The familiar is very comfortable.

Very often physical exercise can be helpful when breaking the vegetative state. Meditation can be very helpful if we are moving compulsively. It may also require *chi* (our internal drill sergeant) to be able to exercise when we don't want to or a great deal of self discipline if we need to meditate. We are mind, body, and spirit and those need to be working in harmony for us to be truly happy. When we exercise, the increase in oxygen, dopamine, and norepinephrine (brain chemistry) will help in the inertia-breaking process. Our brain chemistry also can be corrected by meditation (sedentary) when we have been too busy.

The Circle of Connection

The Taoists talk about the *Yin*, which are the receptive forces in nature, and the Yang, which are the more assertive/aggressive forces in nature. When these are working in harmony, they produce a good life. This circle of receptivity and the assertion of energy is important in keeping ourselves balanced as is mentioned above regarding exercise and meditation but also in our relating to others while applying the H.A.L.F.S. principles. Carl Jung wrote about the animus in women, which is their more masculine personality (aggressive), and the anima in men, which is their more feminine (receptive) side. He describes the seemingly masculine features that women have naturally and the more feminine features that men have as a part of their spiritual being. Both men and women need to be both assertive and receptive.

These are the forces of giving and receiving. Both are equally important to good connections which make for a good life. If we love others but will not allow ourselves to be loved, we will not be healthy. If we appreciate others and do not receive the appreciation that others have for us, we will not be healthy. Certainly, to ask and receive forgiveness is essential to our mental health. We clearly need to forgive others so that we are not knotted up with resentments and living in the past. To keep these forces of giving and receiving in balance is not an easy task but one that allows an ethical life to be a good one.

Being Emotionally Healthy is about Relationships

To review: The goals of happiness and self-actualization are all about putting relationships with ourselves and the world around us first. There are five principles that can provide a guide to these relationships. The goal that we "finish first" is a state of happiness and peace. This can be a rather enduring state. However, it will be forever changing in form as we are changing. We may be happy and at peace with a new marriage when we are young or happy and at peace appreciating a beautiful landscape during our retirement. Our connection with ourselves and others can be guided by the same principles even though the people and the situations in our lives are always changing. What is constant are the five principles themselves and a happy self that (most of the time) loves to be alive and at peace.

We need these principles to guide us through all that changes within and around us. Life is always changing. However, we can remain in a state of enduring happiness and peace through thinking about these principles, acting on them, and enjoying the emotions that are the product of this thinking and acting. As our lives change, our peace can be enduring. This is particularly true if we are accepting of the fact that living by the H.A.L.F. principles are leading us to a life of the spirit. It is this spiritual life which can be experienced in our material bodies that endures for a lifetime. I can often hear my younger boy saying to me in my head, "Don't kid yourself, Dad, this world is only the beginning."

Having faith; believing in the beauty of the universe and its influence on us is all important. In all humility, even though we can influence others, we don't control the majority of that universe. However, controlling our own thinking (and thus our actions and feelings) puts us in a position to send messages to those around us which *may* or may not influence how others think, behave, and feel. If we can only feel secure when we are in complete control over our environment, we never can feel secure. This tends to be the case for many of us much of the time. Watching the disasters that occur around the world on the news or going to a funeral of someone we knew well is a reminder of how much of our environment is out of our control. If, however, we have faith in what is out of our control and do our best at self-control (and appreciating our own efforts, by the way), we can feel secure.

Controlling our thinking is difficult sometimes but can be very productive. Totally controlling our environment is impossible. When we attempt to do the impossible, we get anxious and depressed. Without faith that things we can't control will eventually be okay, we also will be anxious and depressed. Of course, we can deny our lack of control over our environment, or maybe use alcohol, drugs, or acting-out behavior to help in this denial process. However, it usually doesn't take long for this process to break down, and we are left often frozen in fear. This is, unfortunately, a very popular approach to life's changes. When we're anxious, we tend to work too much; abuse substances, food or sex; obsess about meaningless details; escape into sleep; and sometimes live in a fantasy world. None of these distractions work well for long, so we continue to be anxious and depressed. Living by the serenity prayer is truly the key to so many emotional problems.

It is unfortunate that people involved in religion, philosophy, and psychology don't communicate with each other more often. This communication between theoretical disciplines is far better than when I was a young college student. At that time, I can remember the intense rivalry between the American University Psychology Department and the Philosophy Department. To me truth is truth. I don't believe that any academic discipline has a corner on wisdom. Ironically, very often, hidden in common phrases or the wisdom of the masses are the profound truths that make us all whole. "Love makes the world go 'round," "God is Love," "Keep it simple, stupid," and many other seemingly trite phrases often contain a great deal of wisdom. Once again, it is important to remain humble and appreciate the wisdom that is all around us. We can learn and teach others from any socio-economic status, at any age if we are truly humble. Commonly used phrases often contain the profound truths that we need to live by. Unfortunately, because intellectual snobbery gets in the way of true humility, we dismiss these nuggets of truth because they seem too simple to be important. This is unfortunate.

Our Goals

I want to reiterate the importance of goals and what many people would say is their most important goal—to be happy and serene. We need goals. It's important that we have the right goals. To me the right goals are all about relationships with ourselves and the world around us. To get this done we have to look carefully at the quality, moment-to-moment, of our ethical and spiritual involvement with ourselves and others, not just our linear or tangible accomplishments such as promotions, salary increases, higher degrees of learning, or similar accomplishments in the world. If I am making a lot of money as a tool to make my and others' lives healthier, then this is a good short-term goal. If I am getting a better education for the purpose of improving the quality of my and others' lives, this is a good goal. If I am feverishly working on either of these goals for recognition or security alone, then these seemingly responsible goals could actually turn into a toxic situation where all the relationships with our inner self and others are severely damaged. Goal achievement at the expense of valuable intimate relationships is a very common source of emotional problems.

It is also of paramount importance that we are able to stay clearly in the present while we are working on these goals, not an easy task. It is so easy to be so wrapped up in the future that we don't consider the here and now, in the moment-to-moment handling of our relationships which actually give wings to our goals. If I am set on writing this book about relationships and forget to pay careful attention to my own relationships with myself and others, not only will I become unhealthy but, most likely, the quality of the writing will also suffer.

For the purpose of clarity, the ethics of the H.A.L.F. principles are applied harmoniously, though I've described them separately in this manuscript. I would like to remind the reader that there are actually five major concepts which I perceive as the foundation for these healthy relationships. The fifth is spirituality. The first four concepts tend to lead to a life of spirituality but not always. This spirituality may not take the form of religion because, unfortunately, some forms of religion or religious thinking actually may keep people from being spiritual. Often when religious thinking loses its humility, it may lose its spirituality altogether.

I was very impressed with the Dali Lama's interview on the Pierce Morgan Show in mid-April of 2012 as he talked about humility. He was frequently praised by Morgan during that interview. In response the Dali Lama kept saying "we are the same." I am also reminded of the historical Jesus who is illustrated as riding on a donkey in spite of thousands of people praising him on Palm Sunday or picturing him sitting Indian style on the ground with children in his lap. These images remind me of the humility of these great leaders. As a matter of fact, I have an image in my head of Jesus, Mohamed, Gandhi, and the Buddha all sitting in a circle, cross-legged on the ground, with small children in their laps It is the humility of these great leaders saying through their actions that we are of equal value that opens their followers to take in completely the lifesaving messages that they to offer.

We must remain humble to be able to take in their teachings. If we are feeling arrogant and have no desire to take in their teachings, it won't happen. If we are self-effacing, we may feel that new knowledge won't help us because of our inadequacy, and we won't take it into our consciousness. Actually, our children, our clients, or the people under our authority can be our teachers or mentors.

Nice People Finish First is about reaching the goal of happiness and serenity, living harmoniously in a loving manner within ourselves and with the world around us. It is not competition that drives the nice people but primarily the desire to live harmoniously. The second we decide to direct our minds to be humbly appreciative of ourselves and others, doing loving things for ourselves and others, and being forgiving of ourselves and others, we have reached our goal of happiness and serenity. In that moment we will have reached our goal and we will be focused on the health of our soul which is eternal. This is true mental health which will sustain us through any tragedy.

Made in the USA
Middletown, DE
09 January 2022

57272646R00146